JOYPADS !

The design of game controllers

Nicolas Nova
Laurent Bolli

Content

Introduction   4

Part 1 - Evolution   16

Part 2 - Gripping   46

Part 3 - Navigation   86

Part 4 - Action   122

Part 5 - Incorporation   156

Conclusion   176

Acknowledgements   184

Bibliography   186

Photos   188

Introduction

In Back to the Future Part II, the movie's main character, Marty McFly, finds himself in 2015 in a bar with two kids in front of an arcade game, Wild Gunman (1974). He tells them how he is unbeatable and starts playing. Picking up the peripheral, the kids exclaim, *"You mean you have to use your hands? That's like a baby's toy!"* Although Wild Gunman is played with a light gun rather than a game controller, this scene is telling us that there is no future for buttons and joysticks. Any physical accessory will be no more than a relic from the past and its use something to be sniggered at.

To come back to our own time, with the "future" described in that film just round the corner, we realize that this situation is not as futuristic as we thought. While standard game controllers are indeed facing competition from other types of peripheral such as accelerometers with Nintendo's Wii, 3D cameras (Microsoft Kinect[1]), or more original devices like headsets to pick up brain waves (Emotiv EPOC, Neurosky Mindwave), there is plenty of mileage still to be got out of the joypad, which may be old hat in the movie but is still a common feature. Consoles are still sold with pads, and keen players insist on using them, actually preferring them to the gestural interfaces.

The iconic status of joypads is also a sign of their importance. Their fairly standard shapes, colors and buttons have gradually become a status symbol for a whole new medium; video games are often represented graphically with a more or less faithful picture of a real game controller. For the gamepad to have become so emblematic in our society means that it has influenced other areas as well. The so-called "directional pad" is now equally to be found on appliances other than toys (e.g. remote controls sold with Wifi boxes, or interactive in-flight equipment); and even the US Army has developed an interface to guide its drones and missiles with PlayStation 2 Dual Shocks! The advent of motion sensors may be

---

1 - With regards to console naming, we shall try as far as possible to use only the name of the first model brought out in the device's home country (Famicom, Super Famicom, Kinect).

seen as a new direction in game peripheral evolution, although we note a smooth progression in Nintendo Wii and Sony Move game controllers; far from making a break with what was previously on offer, their buttons, visual codes and names are similar to the earlier gamepads. A cursory glance shows for instance how the Wiimote is not so very different from the original Nintendo console that came out twenty-five years earlier. If you take a Famicom controller (1983), stretch it somewhat and add on a few extra buttons, you only have to rotate it through ninety degrees to get from one to the other.

For all their importance in the video games culture, joypads generally come in for less close scrutiny than the platforms or the games. In the press and specialist blogs, very often there will be more interest in a machine's capabilities, the relevance of new releases or what game designers think of the controllers. The academic literature in the disciplinary field of game studies is directed preferentially at the analysis of games and consoles[2] and/or their social or cultural implications. This leaves the books and files presenting the old console models or forum discussions among players, going hammer and tongs at each other over the relative merits of this pad model compared with that one. To find a grain of information on the history of game controllers, all that is left are just a few specialist books from publishers like Retro Gamer (UK), Pix'n Love (France), and the odd post on someone's blog.

This is all the more surprising since controllers are a key element in the relationship that users build with games. Whether held in the hands or angrily thrown to the floor, the joypad is the crucial link between the player and their machine. It is the physical interface that lets you interact with by definition intangible computer programs. This indeed is what makes them so interesting. Correctly designed and adapted, they give users this feeling of immersion and fine control that makes the game experience such an intense one. Transformed, renewed, modified with each new console model, these changes the pads come in for accompany successive generations of game hardware and mechanisms. The value

2 - See for instance Ian Bogost and Nick Montfort, Racing the Beam: The Atari Video Computer System, MIT Press, 2009.

of joypads lies then in their nature as an object on the borderline
between industrial design (the controller as a tangible object) and
interaction design (the controller as an interface controlling an object appearing in the digital world).

Given this distinctive feature, they can then be viewed as a
singular artifact providing its own slant on the history of video
games... and hence deserving our attention. So, taking it as an
entry point, this book describes how this object came into being
and how various social, gaming and technical factors have had an
effect on it over time. More specifically, we will be looking into the
following questions: how did joypads appear? To what extent have
video games had an impact on their evolution? Why do they have
this characteristic shape? Where did the directional pad and the
various buttons come from? Are there any elements external to the
video game culture that have had an influence on game controllers
per se? How did the gamepad come to take over from the joystick?
Lastly, in this age of gestural interfaces, what future does this peripheral have?

To answer these questions, we shall be obeying the French
writer Georges Perec's suggestion to "question [y]our teaspoons"[3]
by focusing on a supposedly ordinary item of our everyday lives in
order to question, observe and analyze its specific aspects. This is
what we shall be doing here in addressing the history of the video
game from the standpoint of one of its most overlooked components, the game controller.

With this approach in mind, this book has three aims:

To provide a descriptive view of the object; the analysis of the
various game controllers and the career of joypads during their
brief existence will demonstrate just how complex their design actually is. As shown in Figure 1, the succession of "official" models
produced by the console manufacturers (Nintendo, SEGA, Atari,
Sony, Microsoft), spread over the last thirty years, offers a diversity and continuity that we shall be exploring in detail. The more
exotic models proposed by peripheral designers (Logitech), third

3 - Georges Perec, L'Infra-ordinaire, in Species of Spaces and Other Pieces, London, Penguin Books, 1999, p. 210.

party publishers (Namco) or plain copies (Vii) will also take us down some more unlikely or unfamiliar paths.

To contribute an explanatory view: why does a joypad look the way it does? What decisions were taken that make the different models look so alike? What are their main design features? As emphasized by a philosopher of engineered objects like Gilbert Simondon: "you cannot invent just anything, anywhere, at any time and anyhow: matter imposes its own constraints"[4]. We shall see how starting from basic problems (how to manage movements, have a varied range of actions, offer enough versatility to play different types of games), different solutions have been envisioned, converging on very similar models.

To bring out an overall viewpoint: what does this say about the history of interfaces and engineered objects? Can "evolutionary laws" be derived from them? This analysis may also be seen as a way of decoding what game controllers tell us about the video game culture, or more generally about computer interfaces.

To achieve these goals, this book relies on two types of sources. We rely first on factual data obtained in interviews with game controller designers and the makers of video games, and on a bibliography dedicated to this subject. This bibliography includes historical documents, patents and scientific publications. Secondly, we have built up a collection of game controllers (both official and otherwise), pictured in the central section. This will enable us to analyze the joypads and make comparisons between models according to various parameters: their general shape, navigation interface, action buttons etc. This exploration will also lead us to identify subgroups evolving in different ways. If we take the example of the directional pad (d-pad), it is easy enough to highlight "diverging lines" between the models by Nintendo (solid cross) and Sony (cross divided into 4 arrows). Documentary research completes this approach, separating models into lines by technical principle and by date of appearance. By identifying these genealogies, we shall build up "family trees" evidencing different trajectories. In this way we can describe the changes in straightforward

4 - Gilbert Simondon, Du mode d'existence des objets techniques, Persée, 1958.

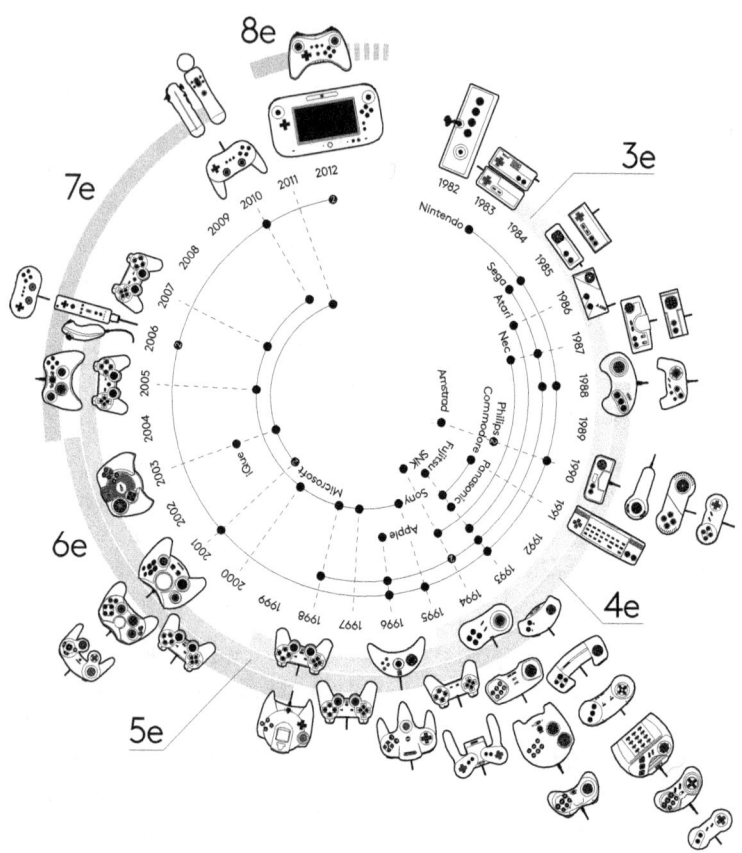

Figure 1: timeline of the official models

terms and show how certain design choices have "done the rounds" over time.

The originality of the analysis put forward in this book is also based on a number of principles underlying our investigation.

First of all, we regard it as fundamental to avoid focusing on any one controller, but rather on the historical sequence composed of the succession of models, from the oldest traceable entities up to the very latest cases. No game controller is a separate, isolated accessory; each is part of a trajectory that can be revisited, and its ancestors and its origin explored. Bearing this in mind, we shall be operating like a paleontologist ordering fossils in relation to each other. In this way we shall reconstruct changes over time on the basis of the models that we have collected. The evolution of engineered objects bears many similarities with that of living beings, if we except autonomous development or the ability to reproduce without human help[5]! The idea behind this reference to evolutionary theory here is rather as a relevant mode of organization for describing engineering trajectories and modifications over time.

As this work to reconstruct this family tree advances, we shall also be considering game controllers as "embedded" objects that can thus be broken down into basic building blocks[6]. To understand this notion, you only have to take a joypad like the Sony Dual Shock and take it to pieces. As shown in Figure 2, the controller is made up of a set of primary engineered elements: a plastic shell in two halves, a plate with the electronic components, a motor, and an array of buttons (17 on the PS3), with wires to connect them all together. Each of these components included in the pads may be seen as a choice made by the game designers and controller manufacturers. Their presence, position and role in controlling games may be understood as the players' ability to act in concrete form. To offer a d-pad and to put it on the left is to give users a means of moving around, but it is also to do so in a manner similar

---

5 - For a more "academic" discussion of this subject, see Stephen Jay Gould, The Panda's Thumb. More Reflections in Natural History. Norton & Company, 1980.

6 - For a discussion of such breaking down see the notion of "cultural elements" by Basile Zimmermann in Materiality, Description and Comparison as Tools for Cultural Difference Analysis, in Companion to New Media Dynamics, 2013.

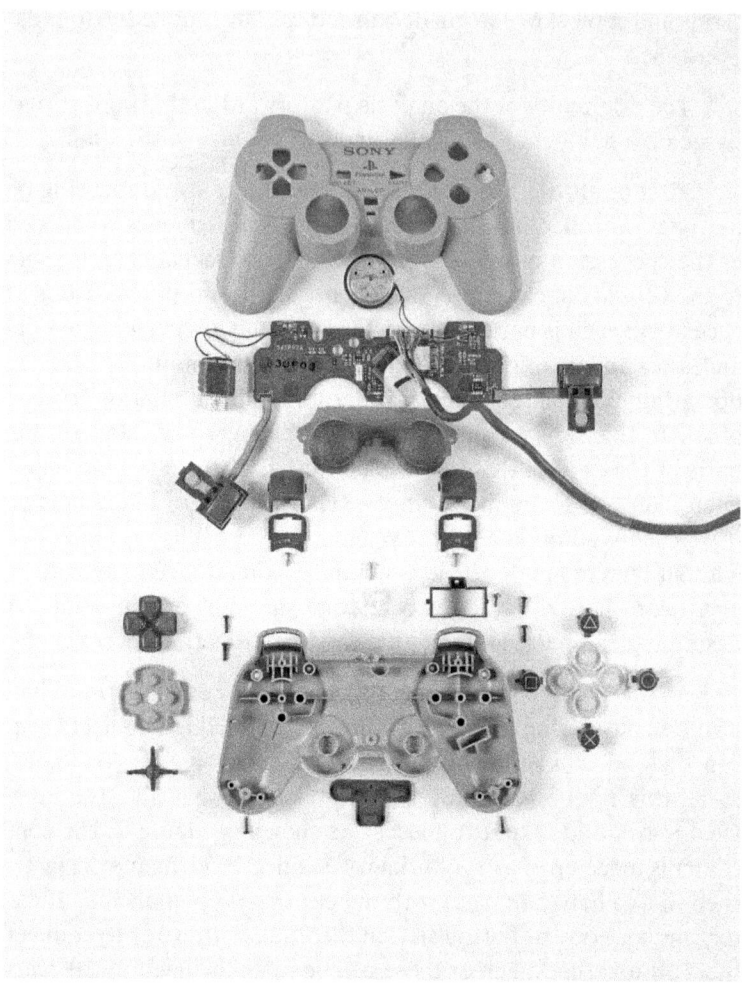

Figure 2: Sony Dual Shock game controller dismantled.

to the ancestor of the video game, namely the arcade game, which mostly had the joystick on the left. Hence the pad may be said to sum up the game designers' intentions, the way they imagine the users and the interactions they intend for them[7].

Because of this, our analysis will take place at a more detailed level than just an examination of the joypads per se; we shall be looking at the changes affecting each of the components—the d-pad cross (in the chapter on game navigation), the shape of the pads (in the chapter on gripping) or again the various action buttons (in the chapter so named). Going down into this level of detail will enable us to be more precise than the host of genealogies to be found on the Internet. Also, such a reconstruction of the evolution of these basic building blocks taken one at a time will give us an insight into how these design choices have circulated, their persistence, and any modifications or discontinuations over time; why does the d-pad nearly always feature? Why do joysticks disappear and then make a "come-back" in miniaturized form?

Finally, the last principle we adopt, given the diversity of video games peripherals, and the wealth of material collected in connection with them, we have chosen to restrict our examination to joypads only. They form a consistent set of objects, making our comparative analysis more relevant than were we to include guns, joysticks, steering wheels or fishing rods. This is because by limiting ourselves in this way, it is easier to investigate the family tree in greater depth and dissect their evolution in minute detail.

Joypad?

On this subject, this being the central theme of the book, it is time to define exactly what we mean by "joypad" or "gamepad", and to pinpoint what sets it apart from other engineered objects. From a general standpoint, it is an interface providing "remote control" of a video game, i.e. at a distance from the output peripheral, which is the screen. As the TV sets and the computer monitors around at

7 - What the sociologist of techniques Madeleine Akrich calls a "script" in her article The De-Scription of Technical Objects", in Bijker, W.et Law, J., ed, Shaping Technology/Building Society. Studies in Sociotechnical Change, MIT Press, 205-224 (1992).

the start of the video games story came with just a few buttons to switch channels, designers had to devise a suitable control mechanism. This later came to be called the "joypad" or "game pad".

So a joypad is a remote control enabling the user to manipulate a computer program. In most cases, the pad is used to operate a very specific type of application: video games. But diversification being the name of the game, throughout their history joypads have also been put to other uses. Think for instance of the Philips CD-i remote, or the PS3 pad, a veritable multimedia control interface for viewing photos, playing films or Web browsing. In addition, the control operated from the joypad by the user is achieved by converting mechanical actions (pressing a button, or tilting a stick in a given direction) into digital instructions through the electronic components inside the controller.

And then, compared with other computer control interfaces, the joypad has two distinctive features. What first strikes us is its silhouette. The word pad suggests both a rectangular block (as in writing pad) and something to absorb shocks (padding). In the early days of game consoles, Nintendo's Famicom or the SJ-300 from SEGA ("Service Games") had game controllers with looks to account for this name. So this unity of shape is an obvious clue: from the NES brick to the ergonomic block of the Dual Shock held in both hands, a joypad is instantly recognizable. Basically what has happened is that this brick shape has turned into something rounder, a snug fit in the hands. While some of them move away from this standard appearance, we shall nevertheless be looking at some recent "remote" type games accessories such as the Wiimote or the Sony Move Navigation Controller. It is because they follow on directly from earlier gamepads, and may be seen as a game controller divided between the two hands that they can be included in this category. The second feature that needs to obtain for a peripheral to be described as a gamepad is quite simply the functional standpoint, namely what the player is actually controlling with this interface. Generally speaking, a joypad is made up of two blocks, sometimes three. You find, usually on the right, a way of commanding a character or object to move around the screen: with the d-pad or analog sticks. On the left or on the side are a set of action buttons or triggers. These both control what happens on the screen (firing a gun, jumping) and manage operation of the device (stopping a game, turning up the sound). Lastly, you have ways to manipulate the mode of representation, notably the viewing angle for the character on screen and their surroundings in 3D games (camera controls). This last type of interface is not systematic and is only found on post-Nintendo 64 (N64) game controllers.

With this set of features, we see how a model building remote control is not a joypad, and neither is the TV remote in your living-room. Historically speaking, if we follow this definition, the earliest proper pad would be Nintendo's Famicom (1983). Likewise the Vectrex and the Intellivision game controllers are not joypads since they predate the d-pad. Hence we shall not be including arcade sticks in this book (on account of their different shape!), portable console interfaces (even though they look very like joypads), nor everyday objects turned into game peripherals (steering wheels, floor mats etc.). However, we will be taking an occasional look at other game controllers such as joysticks or paddles on the basis that these have had a crucial influence on pads.

Book structure

This book is not an encyclopedia, nor is it a catalogue. In this regard, we shall not be going into the details of each and every console and its game controller, for two reasons. First, because our aim is to cover the key moments in the story of joypads, and secondly because, like any historical overview, documents are not always available about each model and their history! Also, we shall only be mentioning games that have had a marked influence on the controllers themselves.

Rather than a chronological description, analyzing game controllers for each generation of consoles, the book offers a succession of chapters on the factors that have influenced joypad evolution and joypad component circulation over time. Each of the five sections will describe how game and controller designers have made some specific choices leading to various shapes and interfaces. Depending on the chapter and the importance of certain makes and designers, we shall be looking at the landmarks in the history of video games.

In Chapter One, we shall be covering the history of game peripherals in the pre-gamepad era, in order to show how past decisions have had an effect on game controller design with the first home consoles. We shall go all the way back to the earliest video game interfaces on the oscilloscopes and computers of the 1950s, highlighting the circulation of certain principles introduced from other areas such as aviation, physical measurement or pinball machines.

This introduction will be followed by a second chapter dealing with the evolution in game controller shapes and gripping, i.e. how we grasp objects in our hands. We shall look at the reasons for choosing the brick shape and things explaining the increased streamlining over time.

Chapter Three will describe how in video games navigation resources have led to some original options such as the directional pad or the revival of analog sticks. We will see how games mechanics and the technical possibilities in terms of graphic effects, from 2D to 3D, have played a key role in this evolution, and why the d-pad has become a standard feature that is here to stay.

The actions available to players are a basic parameter that is covered in Chapter Four. To design a video game is to leave users with the opportunity to do a certain number of things in a digital world. And that necessarily involves physical resources on the game controller. In this section, we will be examining the increasingly complex things that players can do and how this has been translated into the different generations of joypads.

Chapter Five will look at the way game controllers have incorporated more and more functions over their history: storage medium, feedback through vibrations or even control monitor. This part will also be an opportunity to go through a few other engineered objects that have been hybridized in pads: things like keyboards, heartbeat sensors and fans will be our examples in showing the broad range of this artifact.

Lastly, to wrap things up, we shall end with the lessons to be drawn from the evolution of joypads and what they have to say about the history of video games and computing.

Part 1 - Evolution

The first way to understand the joypad as a video gaming interface involves reconstructing its genealogy as one of several control peripherals. While the game controller has been a distinct artifact recognizable as such for thirty years now, it nonetheless needs to be viewed as the outcome of a development based on several forerunners.

As is often the case with technological innovations, it is hard to settle on a unique starting point to the history of the video game. This sector emerged simultaneously during the second half of the 20th century in a number of Western research laboratories, until it became a global industry. And to do this, they found inspiration in earlier games formats or control interfaces in fields as far apart as electrical measurement and aviation.

In this chapter, we shall be reconstructing joypads by tracing them back to their commonest ancestors. Each of these is based on different engineering principles leading to distinct game types.

Playing with video

What forms the common denominator of the video game's "ancestors" is the principle of controlling visual elements on a screen by offering a potentially fun challenge to the player or players. Unlike nowadays, back in the 1950s, the only possible output peripheral involved using the early calculator monitors found in research laboratories, or those machines enjoying increasing commercial success: TV sets. These were the two directions actively taken by various engineers in both the USA and the UK.

In the history of computers, the pioneer scientists in this area looked at chess from the theoretical standpoint of artificial intelligence. Thus in 1947, Alan Turing developed a machine that played chess on paper, and then with a prototype calculator. Later, in 1950, in an article entitled "Programming a computer to play chess", Claude Shannon described how a set of coded instructions might defeat a human chess player. Without downplaying this groundbreaking research, these examples from the early period of computing remind us how in those days it was a theoretical discipline, in which researchers set about tackling mathematical issues before designing user interfaces. Here the game was seen not as an end in itself but rather as a situation through which to understand how a program could solve a problem that it was set.

Intended more for the general public, the Nimrod computer, built by the UK corporation Ferranti International, included a game of strategy called "Nim" for the Festival of Britain's Exhibition of Science in 1951. Back then, this program was intended to demonstrate the Ferranti's impressive computing power. The machine in question was huge in size because of all the flashing valves used to represent the game's visual appearance, and the Nimrod's control peripheral then comprised a table made up of seven times three buttons (replicating the valve matrix). It was also around this time that the first computers came out with a more sophisticated video display than the simple oscilloscope. These were designed, inevitably in the Cold War years, to calculate trajectories for modeling ballistic missile launches. This did not prevent Charles Adama, at MIT in 1950, from inventing the "Bouncing Ball", developed for the Whirlwind Computer, with its video monitor displaying text and graphics in real time. On the other hand, it was not yet a game since participants could not interact with the ball. However, it was one of the rare examples of a computer with an output channel understandable by a human user, namely video, and not just a set of flashing lights.

In a similar vein, we should also mention the "Noughts and Crosses" project developed by a PhD student called Alexander Douglas at the University of Cambridge (England) in 1952. In it the familiar game was adapted for the Electronic Delay Storage Automatic Calculator (EDSAC) fitted with a cathode ray tube display. Owing to the presence of a graphic representation on a 35 by 16 pixel matrix, this may be said to have been the first ever video game in the strict sense of the word. The player played against the machine by specifying the box they wanted to fill with a cross by entering the corresponding number with the EDSAC's mechanical telephone dial; so this device was used the way we use a keyboard. Although subsequently this interface was not employed much[8], this is a classic example of the alternative uses hardware could be put to, which is central to the advent of the video game.

Douglas's work is crucial in the history of computing because he was one of the first to tackle what was a whole new dimension in those days, that of interfaces. Indeed, back in the fifties, what was much later on to become the "computer" and was still called a "calculator", had the appearance of huge electronic cabinets with which the users interacted via cables and switches. The advent of screens, and later control peripherals, was a major step forward in the search for interfaces more accessible to human participants. Thus Alexander Douglas, followed by other pioneers, people like Douglas Engelbart (mice) and Ivan Sutherland (graphic interfaces) contributed to this field with their various inventions.

The few afore-mentioned instances show us how even back then scientists at technology R&D laboratories were using games as investigation tools. The issues they were working on could be addressed from various different angles. But to simulate a bouncing ball or work out the reasoning that a machine was required to perform in order to outplay a human user in the game of chess were ways of making progress with more general issues facing computing and artificial intelligence. So the video game may be said to have been a, by nature unexpected, fringe benefit of the advent of electronic calculators, computers and broadly speaking the technological research conducted during the Second World War and the Cold War period. By developing platforms later taken over by do-it-yourself researchers and engineers, the military industrial complex often provided the early video games designers with the technical basis and sometimes the imaginative aspect, a point we shall come back to.

Despite their innovative character, computer-based projects were of necessity restricted to laboratories since these machines were not available to the general public—back then they were not just huge, they were hugely expensive as well. Not so the television

8 - Outside of Japanese projects such as "Capcom's Forgotten World", in 1992.

set; TVs were produced in the post-Second World War period for a mass market in the US. While 0.5% of the population of the USA owned a set in 1946, by the end of the fifties this figure had soared to 90%. And naturally enough, this new technological data point encouraged some people to extend the possibilities of television so that viewers could play a more active part in the content offered on the screen.

Despite the small number of TV sets at the end of the war, the earliest example of an electronic game was a project called the "Cathode Ray Tube Amusement Device"[9]. Dating from 1945, it was made by Thomas T. Goldsmith Jr. and Settle Ray Mann for Dumont, an American TV channel pioneer. This was a torpedo launcher simulation inspired by World War II radars and presented on a TV screen. The players had to fire missiles at a target (an aircraft) stuck directly onto the screen. Goldsmith and Mann's electronic circuitry used the cathode ray tube to draw the projectile's trajectory and create an explosion around the target whenever it was hit. The controller peripheral was no more than a knob to set the firing angle. Although a patent application was filed for this device in 1947, Dumont never released a commercial version of this project.

The other landmark case of a TV game was produced in 1951 by a 29-year-old engineer called Ralph Baer. As a German refugee in the United States during the war, Baer was among the first students to gain the newly created wireless and television technician's diploma. In the early 1950s, his then employer, Loral Electronics, a supplier to the US Army, asked him to take part in a project to design an original upmarket television set. *"We used test equipment to check our progress and one of the pieces of equipment we used put horizontal lines, vertical lines, cross-hatch patterns, and color lines on the screen. You could move them around to some extent and use them to adjust the television set. Moving these patterns around was kind of neat and the idea came to me that maybe we wanted to build something into a television set. I don't know that I thought about it as a game, more something to fool with and to give you something to do with a television set other than to watch stupid network*

9 - U.S. patent #2.455.992: CRT Amusement Device.

programs.[10]" However attractive it may have sounded, the Loral management had other ideas and it was dropped, on the grounds that the television project must not be held up. Nonetheless, these experiments enabled Baer to explore the bases for what was later to become the video game. He subsequently returned to this field, as we shall see, as the designer of the first ever commercial model of a game console.

The examples mentioned in this section basically represent no more than the first tentative steps made by video games, a term that is barely appropriate when referring to them—whether because some (the Bouncing Ball) offered no user participation in any shape or form, or because these games were just fiddling around with R&D projects or research tools serving some other end purpose (artificial intelligence programming) or to communicate how powerful the tool was. But most of all, the lack, strictly speaking, of any video signal meant that the prototypes produced were sketchy affairs[11]. So we now come to the first game projects going beyond these very early stages, and take a closer look at the different types of interfaces offered to players to control the game.

From the oscilloscope to control knobs

One of the first engineered lines from which the video game originates was taken from Tennis for Two developed at Brookhaven National Laboratory in 1958. A forerunner of Pong, this prototype simply simulated a tennis rally with a knob and a button connected to an oscilloscope screen.

William A. Higinbotham, one of the researchers at this lab, based on Long Island on the United States east coast, had noticed how visitors found the center's annual open day excruciatingly dull and boring. Most of the fare was scientific diagrams, photos and maps deliberately blurred so as to avoid divulging the exact location of nuclear sites across North America. Now Higinbotham,

10 - Tristan Donovan, **Replay: The History of Video Games**, Yellow Ant, 2010.

11 - The term "video" in "video game" does indeed imply that the electronic signals coming from the device later called the "console" are converted into images on a screen with a raster scanning system.

who had previously worked on the detonator of the first A-bomb, and felt critical and resentful with regard to that technology, also happened to be a great fan of the arcade games of the day, namely pinball tables.

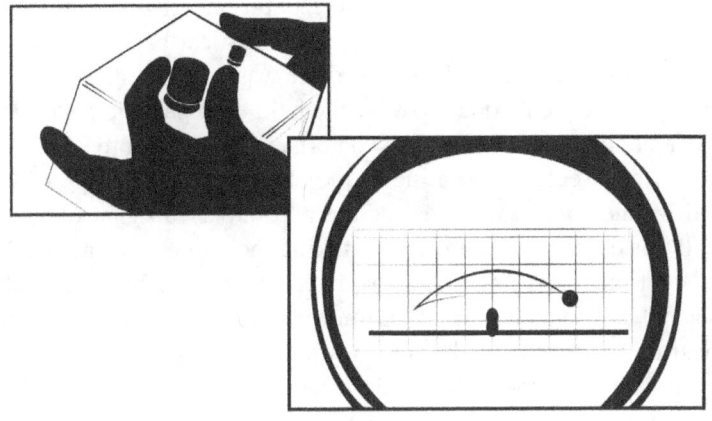

Figure 3: Tennis for Two (1958)

So, to make the visit to the center a more enjoyable experience, he decided to design an interactive show using whatever hardware came to hand: *"It occurred to me that it might liven up the place to have a game that people could play, and which would convey the message that our scientific endeavors have relevance for society."[12]* After reading in a ballistics manual that a computer could be used to calculate a missile's flight path, he and his colleague Robert V. Dvorak decided to modify this program to devise a tennis simulation on an oscilloscope: *"the instruction booklet that came with this analog computer described how to generate various curves on the cathode-ray tube of an oscilloscope, using resistors, capacitors and relays. Among the examples were the trajectory of a bullet subject to gravity and wind resistance, ICBM trajectory and a bouncing ball. The latter suggested the tennis game."[13]* This is a classic

---

12 - Cited in Tristan Donovan, op. cit.

13 - Ibid.

example of creative strategy in video games that involves striking a balance between some technical possibility (the interfacing of the oscilloscope with its potentiometers) and an existing game concept (the game of tennis).

Based on a side-view of a tennis court, game participants had to get a ball to bounce along a horizontal line placed at the foot of the screen, while avoiding the short vertical bar representing the net—no easy task, given that there was nothing on the screen to represent the racquets! To hit the ball, each participant held in their hand an aluminum box comprising a knob (potentiometer) and a push-button. Rotating the knob changed the angle of the ball's trajectory, while pressing the button played the stroke. The ball was extremely rudimentary, taking the shape of a single point of light on something like a five-inch screen. The box also had a second button on it, a reset button with which to make the ball appear on either side of the screen to play again after the rally was over. The fun aspect to Tennis for Two was obviously very limited, as only the ball and the net were featured on the oscilloscope screen. Added to this was a cruel lack of realism: the ball would just hang in the air until one of the players hit it!

The Tennis for Two game was shown to visitors to the Brookhaven gymnasium open day, on October 18th 1958, and naturally caused a sensation compared with the hardware supplied by the laboratory's other researchers. So much so that the simulation was shown again the following year, before ending up being dismantled, to recover the parts for other projects.

While this spelt the end for Tennis for Two as a game, this prototype marked the beginning of the knob as an input interface. The game potential of buttons was recognized eight years later at Sanders Associates, in New Hampshire (USA). It was at this military electronics corporation that we again find Ralph Baer, whom we mentioned earlier. Starting in 1966, when he was chief engineer with Sanders' instruments division, Baer decided to create a games device that could be plugged into a TV set. Called the "Brown Box", it was the very first prototype of a video game console. It was with this version that Baer and his colleagues at Sanders filed a patent

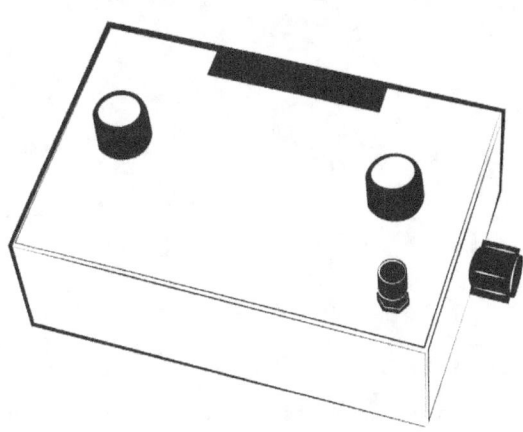

Figure 4: the Brown box game controller

application for a television game device[14]; the application was filed in 1977 but the patent was only granted in 1986.

The originality of Baer and his colleagues Bill Rusch and Bill Harrison's approach lay in the fact that they did not just take over an existing interface on the oscilloscopes of the time. The project also included a proposal for different peripherals, all adapted to each of the actions required by the multiple gameplays available in the programmed games: a box with a potentiometer for playing Ping-Pong, an electric light gun to fire at a target display on the TV screen, a dummy water pump for a firefighter game, etc. While Ralph Baer did not invent the joypad, his pioneering work on the first game console was marked by a number of literal transpositions of everyday objects for a video game peripheral, a trend that crops up several times in the course of history.

As shown in the illustrations taken from the patent application, Baer and his colleagues felt the need to separate the central processing unit from an individual control peripheral: *"control unit may be broken up into a master control unit containing the electronic circuits and individual control units containing control knobs, whereby each participants may operate from a position not*

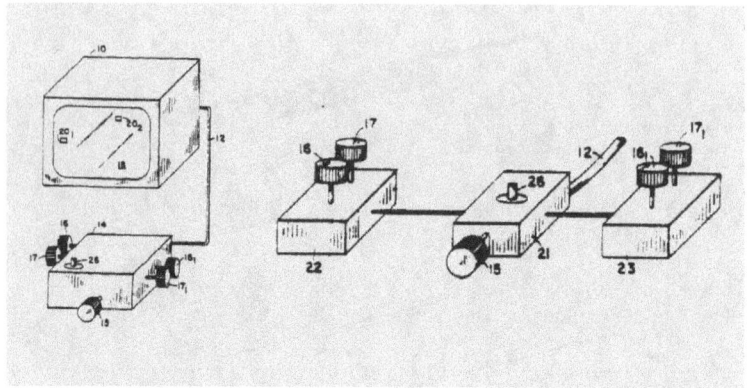

Figure 5: Video game console according to the 1971 patent by Baer and his colleagues at Sanders.

proximate the other and so not to interfere with other players."[15] And this document also indicates in a premonitory fashion[16]: *"The knobs may be combined in a joystick"*, although this particular project had no such embodiment. Figure 5 excerpted from the patent shows the shape given to the game controller at that time; it was more of a pad than the vertical box type that was subsequently chosen. Also the version on the right shows the CPU and the controller as a single entity. In the one on the left, the two are separate.

From the knob to the paddle

Baer and his colleagues' Brown Box remained a secret for a long time. This television gaming project later went public once the Pentagon had shown no interest in this type of appliance. The experts at the American Defense department having judged that this type of technology had very little military potential, Sanders and Baer's team were allowed to develop a commercial product based on the early prototypes. After various refusals on the part of television manufacturers (RCA, General Electrics, Sony, etc.),

---

15 - Ibid.

16 - And this is because analog sticks are the engineered outcome of combining knobs and switches.

Magnavox was the first company to take out a license for this unusual product. Renamed Skill-O-Vision and later Odyssey, brought out in August 1972, this was the first ever commercial model of a video game console.

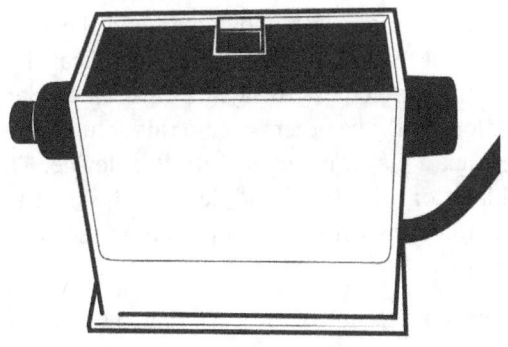

Figure 6: The Odyssey console game controller (Magnavox)

It comprised a terminal to plug into the television and two boxes with which to play from a distance away from the set. Each of these "game controllers" was a plastic box with a "Start" button on the upper edge to launch a game, coupled to two notched knobs. On the right-hand side, the knob marked "vertical" controlled the vertical motion of the object on the screen. On the left-hand side, two knobs were fitted one inside the other; the first one, the same size as the previous one, was called "horizontal" for the horizontal motion and the second marked "ball" to serve the ball in the tennis (Ping Pong) and hockey games, the main ones using this peripheral. Oddly enough, the game design at the time was very confused: playing tennis on Odyssey you could move your racquet in every direction on the screen, including moving into the opponent's court, or hitting the ball with the reverse side of the racquet! Notice how the side knobs were, in electronic language, rotary dials: as on the old telephone dial, rotation was not smooth and direct, it clicked through a number of notches, giving a jerky feel whenever the user turned the knob.

If we look closely at this game controller, we notice how the box was organized with its three buttons in such a way that to control movements around the screen players had to use both potentiometers simultaneously. As the designer Ralph Baer ironically emphasizes, the issue was as follows: *"The two hand controls have three knobs on them, which means you have to have three hands to play them".*[17] Unlike the later, post-Famicom joypads, both hands were needed to handle objects moving around the screen: moving the Ping Pong bat meant turning both the "vertical" knob and the "horizontal" knob. Needless to say, it was even harder to use the third knob along with the other two! So this setup limited the possible things that a player could do with this device. This problem was solved later on with the d-pad, leaving the right hand free to perform other actions with buttons placed on the right-hand side of the gamepads.

Moreover, on account of the fact that the presence of these two side potentiometers, Odyssey users generally had to play while holding the box on a support, otherwise it was liable to slip out of their hands. The photos from that period show players doing contortions with the controller jammed against their knee or on a table. As we see, this first game controller design was rudimentary. The two aforementioned problems (disassociation of movements between the two hands, and holding the box) were not solved for some time.

Like any trail-blazing pioneer, the Magnavox Odyssey console both caused envy and laid down several gaming principles in the collective imagination (sports simulation, opposition between two players, limited to simplified actions). And when Nolan Bushnell, who founded the young California company Atari, asked Al Alcorn, one of his new staff members, to program a very basic game to familiarize people with the arcade machine that he had just created, he described to him the Ping-Pong game that he had seen operating on the Odyssey a few months previously. Bushnell did not want to do anything in particular with this program, as it was merely an exercise he was giving to his young employee. But the highly motivated Alcorn ended up producing a much more sophisticated game than the one he was asked for. So Bushnell was

17 - http://classicgaming.gamespy.com/View.php?view=Articles.Detail&id=386

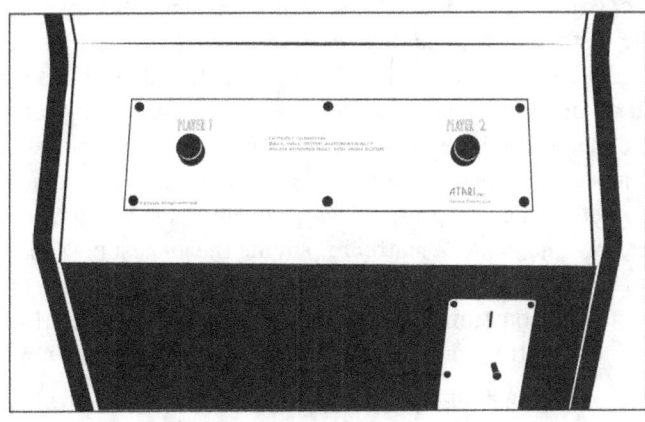

Figure 7: Pong arcade machine control knob

convinced of the value of the program, and renamed it Pong (1972); and he sought to produce the corresponding arcade machines, after pinball giants like Bally Midway turned it down. With a project like this, a phenomenal success story in the history of video games, Bushnell and Atari contrived to move the video game on from being a hobby for academic geeks to a commercial product deployed on a large scale in shopping malls. After threatening Atari with a lawsuit, Magnavox reached an out-of-court settlement with them to transfer the licence to this tennis game, for the sum of 700'000 dollars.

With regard to interfaces, Pong was the first occurrence of an arcade machine that used neither a joystick (as was the case with Galaxy Game in 1971) nor buttons (unlike Computer Space in 1971) as its control mode. For Pong comprised a screen and two potentiometers, one for each player. The object of the game was not to miss the ball crossing the screen from side to side and which could bounce off the racquet provided it was correctly positioned to receive the projectile. Each potentiometer let you control the racquet's vertical movements; this was an application of Nolan Bushnell's idea of having a game that was instantly accessible with no prior explanation or the need to read any instructions. This he later summed up in the memorable phrase *"something so simple that any drunk in any bar could play"[18]*, a fundamental principle in the history of the video game, meaning in concrete terms the choice of a simple single direction knob as the interface, but most of all an adequate combination with a novel gaming system, and sure enough, unlike with Odyssey tennis, the Pong player could only move their racquet along the vertical axis, with a single potentiometer. Regarding the scoring system, there was a big difference: it was no longer a matter of playing the longest possible rally, but of not missing the ball. In addition, the players had to contend with outside constraints, with the ball speeding up over time, requiring extra attention, the winner being the one who did not miss.

As Mathieu Triclot showed in his book "Petite philosophie du jeu video", these very basic principles are at the heart of how arcade games later developed, above and beyond the use of rotary knobs and buttons. To quote a familiar example, Space Invaders (1978) may be seen as a Pong in which the racquet becomes a spaceship, the spaceship moving from right to left, with the potentiometer and an extra button to fire projectiles and destroy these space invaders (racquets) overhead.

The great paddle era

Not content to have turned the video game from a geekish pastime into a mass product for shopping malls, the Atari bosses soon thought up the next step: getting Pong into people's homes. This happened over Christmas in 1975, through a joint venture with the Sears distribution chain for the sale of Tele-game Pong, for playing on television screens. This release led to what Bushnell described in the claim that "It's the first time people have been able to talk back to their television set, and make it do what they want it to do."[19] After this, dozens of brands released Pong clones with electronics companies or even household electrical goods manufacturers (such as Seb in France, with Telescore). Seventeen years after Tennis for Two at the Brookhaven Institute, this was

---

18 - http://boingboing.net/2010/11/08/sons-of-pong.html
19 - The Tuscaloosa News, June 14th 1978.

the first time that the box with the knob entered people's homes and became a game interface on the mass market. As it was a kind of ping-pong bat hitting a ball, the name "paddle" was chosen to describe the game's interface.

With the success of the Pong clones, the designers at Atari realized that a logical sequel to this project would be a device with which to play in several different ways, not just one. This was "Stella", which later became the VCS (Video Computer System) when it came out in 1977, then the Atari 2600 in 1982. This seemed to them the obvious course and earlier experiments with the Magnavox Odyssey console and Fairchild Semiconductor's Channel F had shown the way. But Atari saw it as a high-risk venture, so to pull it off, the company sold itself to the Warner media group. From the outset, the aim of this console project was two-fold: to emulate the success of existing arcade games while insuring a certain amount of versatility. Translating these two aims into input interfaces, this means that the peripherals offered had to allow the various types of games already existing to be played, as well as others yet to come. The solution available in those days for playing several types of games was straightforward enough: you had to have several interfaces. That is what Magnavox had done with their Odyssey console, with one peripheral per game. For the VCS, Atari opted for two: the joystick and the paddle. We shall come back to the former in the section of this chapter devoted to it.

The VCS came with two paddles. Smaller than the joystick, they had just one knob turning through a fixed angle of 330 degrees, with two stops to prevent complete rotation. These paddles also had a red button on the side, with which, inter alia, to accelerate the ball in Pong or throw it in a brick-breaking game. This type of interface was suitable for playing games on the VCS, which needed to control the movements of an object on the screen along a single fixed axis. This was the case with Pong as we have already seen, but also with the well-known brick-breaking game Break-Out (1976) or the sports games Video Olympics (1977). However the designers at Atari soon encountered a problem using the paddle with the new games they were devising. And unlike their colleagues in charge of Odyssey, they could not bring themselves to offer two potentiometers on a single pad, an inefficient combination leaving no fingers free to use anything else. The paddle was seen to be over-restrictive; since it did not have the versatility available with the joystick, for one, it fell by the wayside, so much so that the versions of the console that were sold afterwards, like the Atari 2600 Jr. and the Atari Flashback 2, all came with just the joysticks.

So it was between 1958 (Tennis for Two) and 1977, with the launch of the Atari VCS, that the potentiometer/paddle enjoyed its hour of glory. It then disappeared as such, only making occasional comebacks as an accessory. We may think for instance of the porting of Arkanoid DS on the Nintendo DS, with a small potentiometer that was connected to the portable console's GBA port. Built on similar technical lines, the car race driving steering wheels are another more elaborate version of the paddle, on a bigger scale.

Limited to interactions in one direction only, the paddle is a prime example of an extinction in the history of computer and video game interfaces. From a technical standpoint, however, it was interesting for the continuity of the actions it offered; you could keep turning it to move an object on the screen. Later on, this continuity was added to the joystick to produce the analog stick detecting continuous movements. We shall come back to this later. On the game level, the gameplays that it has allowed are central to video game history, since recent products like Angry Birds (2009) owe a great deal to Pong and to Tennis for Two! This is a good illustration of how even though the interface per se has disappeared, the actual game principle has "circulated" and may subsequently reappear.

The Spacewar! switches

While the knob is the oldest video game interface, a second archetype also played a key role in the early days in this field: the good old electric switch, enabling a choice to be made between two or more positions (generally ON/OFF). We find this in another seminal project: Spacewar! Created at the Massachusetts Institute of Technology (MIT) by Steve Russell and his colleagues Wayne Witanen and J. Martin Graetz in 1961, like Tennis for Two, this game is frequently cited as being one of the pioneering experiences - all the more since it was seen as the symbol of the early days of the hacker movement, with engineers excited at the possibility of diverting an existing machine for their own purposes.

Developed on the PDP-1, a computer made by DEC, Spacewar! was designed to meet the technical constraints imposed by the machine: a screen in the form of a cathode ray tube and a switchboard set vertically in front of the user. At the time, Russell and his colleagues were motivated by the possibility of diverting the PDP-1's realtime display, a first in computing history, to create something original... such as a demonstration program plugged into this function.

The gaming principle adopted by the team was that of a battle in space between two spaceships on either side of a screen representing a sector of the Milky Way. Each controller could fire torpedoes, try to avoid being on the receiving end, and trigger the "hyperspace" function to suddenly disappear and reappear randomly someplace else, evading enemy attacks in the process. The players had to control the ship with the switches on the control board. As explained by Paul Wexelblat, who used to use a copy of Spacewar! at BBN Cambridge: *"Control was accomplished using testword switches (I/O instruction readable) the four on the left for one ship, the four on the right for the other [...] BBN outlawed Spacewar occasionally, mainly because switches died. The life of testword switches was shortened by this game."*[20] More to the point, these four switches corresponded to the following actions: rotate the ship clockwise, anticlockwise, accelerate, fire torpedoes. The hyperspace function, a later add-on, was activated by pressing both rotation buttons on the sides.

From the standpoint of the proposed interface, the use of switches was an alternative line to Tennis for Two. No longer do we have the continuous interaction as on an oscilloscope potentiometer, we now have a set of binary choices. The launch torpedo function is activated at specific moments, each time triggering a shot.

So with Spacewar!, we note an increase in the level of

20 - Paul Wexelblat, PDP-1 Spacewar Reminiscences, in BBN, 1993.

complexity, with five type of actions instead of the two in Higin-botham's game. However this is another instant of a dual dynamic that was here to stay in the story of the video game: one part of the peripheral dedicated to moving the object around the screen, another part to the available actions such as firing or jumping into hyperspace as here. Unlike Tennis for Two and many other games later on, Spacewar! did however place the emphasis on navigation, since four out of the five control elements were used to define the spaceship's movements. The device was so popular among players of the game that DEC used it to demonstrate the capabilities of their PDP-1 computers, and ended up pre-installing a version of Spacewar! on every machine they sold after 1962.

Even though the first Spacewar! release fascinated hundreds of students at MIT and Cambridge, where copied versions were doing the rounds on other PDP-1s, the game designers soon realized that there was a problem when playing with the PDP-1 interface: *"Spacewar! worked perfectly well from the test word switches on the console, except that the CRT was off to one side, so one player had a visual advantage. More to the point, with two excitable space warriors jammed into a space meant for one reasonably calm operator, damage to the equipment was a constant threat. At the very least, a jittery player could miss the torpedo switch and hit the start lever, obliterating the universe in one big anti-bang. A separate control device was obviously necessary, but joysticks (our original idea) were not readily available in 1962"[21]*. Also, given the height of the control board, playing for any length of time was painful for users, who had to hold up their elbows. But the major problem lay with the actual interface itself: the switches were positioned with no particular relevance to the actions they produced in the game, and so players had to memorize what each switch did... making games very one-sided in favor of regular players, who were obviously experts, being familiar with the interface.

For this reason, the next version of Spacewar! had a remote control box, with which to play without staying glued to the PDP-1 control console with its array of eighteen switches. It was by mobilizing the expertise they built up in their Tech Model Railroad Club

21 - John Martin Graetz, The Origin of Spacewar!, in Creative Computing, 1981.

(TMRC) that two of Steve Russell's colleagues, Alan Kotok and Robert A. Saunders, developed their "game controller". To make this peripheral, Russell and his TMRC colleagues "requisitioned"

Figure 8: the Spacewar! remote control

various components from nearby classrooms, and TMRC came to stand for "The Midnight Requisition Club". These controllers came in the shape of a small rectangular wooden, later bakelite box, with two metal switches and a button. The button was used for firing torpedoes, while the levers controlled spaceship rotation and acceleration, triggering both simultaneously. Spacewar! with a partner now became a more level playing-field since both players could sit at the same distance from the screen, with the game controllers on their knees.

After the Tennis for Two control box, the Spacewar! remote control was the second ancestor of the video game controller—a set of switches and a button placed in a box held by the player at a distance from the screen. For the same reasons as for the paddle—lack of versatility and the difficulty in combining more than one—this type of engineering principle very soon fell out of favor.

Switch buttons

Along with the paddles and switches, notice how another engineering principle was a regular extra feature to enhance the gameplay: the push-button, based on the principle of the electric switch. Given the origin of the interfaces used by the ancestors of the video game, the presence of buttons comes fairly naturally as a way of enabling the user to act in the digital world: hitting the ball in Tennis for Two, firing in Spacewar!, etc. Thus the button made way for an initial repertoire of interactions—a single press, or "button mashing", which is repeated, sometimes frantic pressing.

The use of buttons in a game situation did not originate with these ancestors of the video game Tennis for Two and Spacewar!. We also find them in the field of electrotechnical games, of which the pinball machine is the most familiar example. The earliest models of these games thus date back to the beginning of the 19th century. In the form of a wooden crate, they were based on a straightforward principle: the player pressed a button mounted on a spring, to send a ball through a given circuit. Pinball tables evolved, into bigger metal frames, and it was not until 1948 that we saw the first system with two side buttons. Pressing each of these triggered each of the levers, sending the ball back up to the top of the board, thereby enhancing the game. The presence of these buttons gave the player a little more leeway, after initially having to press on the actual front rather than the sides as seen on later models. We again find the use of buttons in another game area based on electricity, namely model building, with histori-cal reproductions of wireless controlled ships, starting in the late 19th century[22].

As push-buttons were one of the standard interfaces on elec-trical appliances and calculators (the ancestor of the computer) after World War II, unsurprisingly they were taken over by the early games designers. From the very beginnings of video games, the button sensing a press of the finger was a crucial interfac-ing feature, rising to even greater prominence with the early ar-cade games, which sometimes had no other control mechanism. This was the case with the first version of the Computer Space (1971) machine developed for Nutting Associates by Nolan Bush-nell. With its avant-gardist look, it offered a control panel with

22 - U.S. patent #613809: Method of and Apparatus for Controlling Mechanism of Moving Vehicle or Vehicles.

buttons only for firing, accelerating and turning in either direction.

The advent of joysticks

Most of the projects we have been talking about so far were conducted in the United States or the UK. But in 1969, another innovation in game interfaces was to come from Japan: the joystick. The first arcade terminal to have offered this control device was called Missile and was developed by SEGA. It was a firing simulator, comprising two directional buttons with which to move a tank and a stick used to direct and fire missiles at aircraft appearing on the screen. This the original joystick however was only a single-direction version moving to right or left but not both.

From this point on, the complexification of mechanical sticks began. 1973 saw the release of the first joystick that could move in four directions, with the Astro Race game (Taito), while in 1978 for Interceptor (Taito) had eight. Whether there were two, four or eight possibilities, for a long time joysticks continued to carry direction indicators in the shape of arrows around the handheld lever.

The use of the joystick then spread to Japanese and North American arcade machines. In particular, it became pre-eminent on this medium with flagship games like Pacman (1980) or Space Invaders (1978), so much so that some games had two of them operating side by side. It was the developer Eugene Jarvis who introduced this type of interface with games like Robotron: 2084 (1982), Ikari Warriors (1986), Battlezone (1980), and Gauntlet (1985). This was a by no means absurd proposition since we still find it nowadays on the PS3 analog sticks on a game like Katamari Damacy (2004).

Technically speaking, a joystick is generally a combination of four switches enabling motion sensing in four directions (up/down/left/right). When the stick is moved up for instance, one of the switches is mechanically activated, generating an electric signal indicating that the player has moved it in that direction. So the joystick is both a throwback from the previous archetype (switches), crossed with an older interface: the joystick used by airmen—the pilot's joystick existed long before video games were even invented.

Before being taken over as a video game interface, the term was indeed in common parlance for around forty years among all kinds of aircraft pilots. The word "joystick", which seems to have been coined by the very early airmen, has several origins considered by the historians of aviation. The term is thought to date back to the early flight control levers invented by the French pilot and engineer Robert Esnault-Pelterie in the early 20th century[23]. It was actually patented by him prior to World War II[24], explicitly using the spelling "joy-stick ". But few sources ascribe the actual coining of the word to him. Be that as it may, this neologism was already beginning to gain currency in 1909, as we find it in the private diary of the English pilot Robert Loraine written in that year at the Louis Blériot air school in Pau (SW France)[25]. Other British pilots and inventors might also be credited with coining the word around the same time. Thus Arthur E. Georges with his G&J (George and Jobling) Company designed a fin control system called the "George stick", which may have been subsequently mispronounced as "joystick".

Above and beyond issues of what to call it, the need to innovate and complexify the mechanics of games accounts for the evolution from simple interfaces (knobs and switches) to the joystick in arcade and console games. By and large, after Pong (1972) or BreakOut (1976), designers felt they needed a control method that was no longer monodirectional; hence the search for solutions to be devised by building on what was already available: combining several switches was seen as an obvious way of gaining extra complexity. The joystick gave the player greater freedom of movement, notably by enabling him to move objects intuitively through more than one dimension[26]. It also led to the notion of "direct manipulation" being democratized in the history of computing: the advent

23 - On this, see Pierre Contensou, L'apport de Robert Esnault-Pelterie, in L'Aéronautique et l'astronautique # 97, 1982.

24 - U.S. patent #330569: Apparatus for controlling land.

25 - Based on the "joystick" entry in the Oxford English Dictionary.

26 - Nick Montfort and Ian Bogost, op. cit.

of the joystick brought a correspondence between a movement through physical space and travel through digital space.

This combination of switches was a major change, later allowing the transition to a second, more elaborate version: the analog joystick. With the standard stick, movements are captured at particular moments by activating switches; hence only four spatial directions can be detected (or two or eight, depending on the number of switches). On the other hand, the analog stick, which appeared later on in pad evolution, added a new feature: you could now have continuity of motion and thus preserve the richness of movements in a way akin to that of an object in physical space. This gave much finer control, as each movement was detected in continuity and not in sudden jerks, as had been the case with the standard stick.

Technically speaking, the analog stick can thus be viewed as a hybridization of two already existing principles: the knob (based on one or more potentiometers), as a mode of sensing movement, and the standard stick, itself descended from the airplane joystick, as a peripheral in the user's hand. This combination of different techniques shows how interfaces and other engineered objects come into being: by juxtaposition then integration.

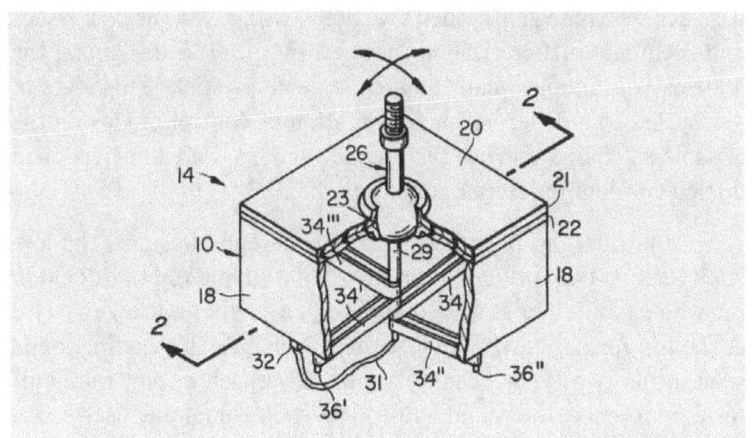

Figure 9: Diagram of the Atari joystick design as presented in the original patent application (filed in 1978)

We first encountered such a system on the Channel F console produced by Fairchild Semiconductor in 1976. With a tube-shaped hand-held detonator, the console controller was fitted with a kind of rotary dial on the top of the cylinder. Rotating this component controlled movements on the screen. But being so small, this knob could not yet be properly described as a joystick—it was more a cross between a paddle and a stick.

The main boost to the popularity of the analog joystick however was the VCS developed by Atari and marketed from 1977 with two sticks fitted with a firing button. As evidenced in the patent application filed by its designer Stephen Bristow[27], the solution he came up with involved a rod attached to a rotary ball whose movement could be detected and converted into an electric signal the variation of which reflected the continuity of the movement imposed by the player. Being so technically versatile, the joystick may be seen as a more "general-purpose" interface than the paddle inasmuch as it could be used to play a broader range of games.

The VCS joystick became so well known in fact that it became synonymous with that era of video gaming and the symbol of retro-gaming, most notably with the release in the early years of the new millennium of versions directly connectable to a TV set, with access to the games then available. Also, given the cost issues and technical difficulties encountered by the VCS designers, the joystick was simpler than the arcade game joystick. This state of affairs led to a different implementation of control modes on the console as compared with the arcade versions, and so players had difficulty adjusting from one to the other.

From then on, both on arcade games and consoles, the joystick took on two forms. First it involved a simple rod to be held in the whole hand, then it was composed of a smaller stick with a ball at the top for handling with just the fingertips. This distinction is seen in the two types of fairly similar joysticks, except for a cultural preference: the round ball-top joystick commonly used in Japan, and the straight bat-top joystick (popular in North America). Another notable oddity is that while most joysticks have the stick

27 - U.S. patent #4091234: Joystick with attached circuit elements.

placed in the middle, there are some arcade games where it is off-center. This was the case with Atari's 720 Degrees (1986), where you could turn the device on its axis to control a character doing figures on a skateboard. Although it was an unusual interface, this configuration made rotations possible very simply and directly.

Notice too how the early arcade game designers had no standard position for the joystick. On the simpler games, the stick was placed in the middle of the machine. But gradually, with the addition of extra buttons, the joystick was moved over to the left side, leaving the right hand free to operate the buttons. As often happens with evolving standards, there were exceptions to this rule, and some game models had a stick on the right and a button on the left. Although designers subsequently abandoned this solution, this detail, as we shall see, was to have its importance with the advent of the directional pad on the joypad.

Figure 10: First ever trackball designed by the DATAR laboratory.
Source: Courtesy of Royal Canadian Navy

Despite the profusion of joysticks on arcade machines, they slowly faded, becoming either an optional accessory on some consoles (NES or SEGA Master System), or featuring only on arcade-oriented consoles (Neo Geo) and computer flight simulators. On the other hand, something we shall be coming back to, it made a big comeback in a minimalist, thumb-sized format on the joypad with analog sticks, beginning with the N64.

Trackball

Before closing this chapter on the engineering principles that came before the joypad, we may recall the existence of one last type of interface that was present from the early days of the video game: the trackball. Even before the mouse came in, this device was offered on several occasions as a computer accessory.

Invented in 1952 by a group of Canadian researchers (Tom Cranston, Fred Longstaff and Kenyon Taylor), the trackball was used as a peripheral to control one of the Royal Navy's calculators: the DATAR (Digital Automated Tracking and Resolving). For the user, it was a ball with which they could move objects around a screen, following the movements of the sphere. In this early version, it was actually a pool ball... an amazing example of yet another cross-fertilization between the engineering culture and the world of games.

The use of a trackball as a means to control a game was revived several times through history. The oldest example was the Atari Football game, released in 1978. As described by one of the game's inventors, Michael Albaugh, this interface had the advantage of allowing detection of a continuous, fluid interaction. *"Trackballs were the only rational control for the game because you needed finer control and you needed, I felt, the physicality of the game was an important concept"*. This principle returned later on with various releases like Centipede (1981), Quantum (1982), and most of all, the marble simulator Marble Madness (1984), where there was a direct correspondence between the marble's movements on the screen and the control peripheral. The player had to move the marbles around a game board with all kinds of traps, and could do so fairly naturally by rolling the marble placed in the middle of the arcade machine. Despite some rather off-putting disagreements on the trackball issue among its in-house staff, Atari reintroduced it in 1983, with a new version of the interface for the VCS.

While the trackball is a recurring feature on arcade machines, we only find it on one game controller: the Pippin, a game console project produced jointly by Apple and Bandai, and which was a memorable flop for both companies[28]. So far, this is the first and last time that a commercial game peripheral using this engineering principle has been marketed. It is now no longer found outside of art work and belonging to the proud owners of older models.

The bases of the edifice

This historical survey shows the close link between the creation of the video game and the invention of the control peripheral. Designing a gaming interaction on a screen was bound to involve an input interface; either that or you made do with whatever was to hand at the time. This is why various switches, knobs, joysticks and potentiometers were all diverted from their original purpose and given this new lease of life.

During the course of their evolution, gaming interfaces have thus been built up from several earlier devices, mostly coming from two areas: first, the products and resources of research into the technologies used during World War II and the Cold War. These were chiefly oscilloscopes, calculators designed primarily for missile detection, and aircraft joysticks. And secondly, the designers of game controllers and joysticks came under the less down-to-earth influence of earlier forms of games. The pinball machine and the pool table are two major examples of ancestors of the video game inspiring these interfaces. Meanwhile, this twofold influence did not come into play solely with respect to the control peripherals, as the actual games themselves also emerged from these cultures. Ballistics in Tennis for Two, and star wars for Spacewar! are the prime examples. But games with marbles such as Marble Madness (1984) also show how earlier, less militaristic fun and games also left their mark. So, loosely speaking, video games interfaces are the outcome of a blending of these two cultures.

Taking together the multiple engineering principles described

---

28 - One reason being a dearth of available games.

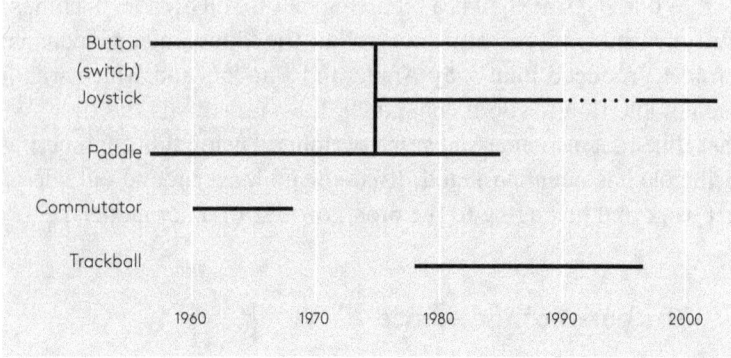

Figure 11: Genealogy of the different video game control engineering principles prior to the advent of the joypad

in this chapter, what do we learn from this "prehistory" of the joypad? We have shown this evolution in diagrammatic form in Figure 11, in which we see the various paths taken by the early game interfaces, and we can draw a few conclusions from this.

The first point is with regard to the constant presence of button-type interfaces; they featured from the outset and have remained popular ever since. This is the stablest archetype, one that demonstrates how invaluable it is in offering a relevant range of actions. Another lesson here is to do with the notion of extinction: the switches used on the very first platforms, along with knobs and trackballs gradually fell by the wayside, either because the interface in question was too restrictive (knob, trackball), or because the hybridization of two of those principles produced something else—the analog joystick, the upshot of combining switches with a knob, or the directional pad, which we shall come to later. Hence old archetypes may either disappear and come back indirectly (the knob on the analog joystick), or disappear for a time, the better to reappear later on (analog sticks on the joypad).

From our analysis of the engineering principles, we may also learn a lesson regarding the types of controller on offer. Generally speaking, you always have a way of moving around (via switches, a knob or a joystick) plus one or more actions via buttons. Thus, alongside the early Pong game or the brick-breaking games, the change from the mono-control scheme to the dual-control scheme with its dual logic of movement and action was fairly rapid. A cursory glance at the early days of the video game shows how interfaces became more complex quite swiftly thanks to such combinations.

In addition, the precursors of video game interfaces highlight a classic debate in usability, namely the choice between peripherals versatile enough to handle several kinds of games (joysticks) and those designed for one particular type (paddles, light guns). As shown in the above genealogy, the survivors would seem to be the devices that do provide this flexibility. Even if our current consoles come with all kinds of accessories, the joypad is nonetheless viewed as being the standard peripheral, designed in such a way that several types of game can be controlled with it. Joysticks and paddles were abandoned because of this lack of versatility.

We may also note that these various different peripherals, and their underlying engineering principles, are quoted as instances of the way to go in order to directly manipulate what happens on the screen. The early days of personal computing were marked by this influence, and in those days, engineers envied the ease with which console users took over these game controllers and what they could do with them on the screen. These game interfaces had a discreet effect on HCI[29] research in those days, because they provided an appropriate and user-friendly design.

The evolution of computer games clearly went hand in hand with the creation of the early computer interfaces, the mouse, keyboard and light pen. These came into being around the same time, and may be seen as a parallel genealogy that later produced its own games forms. We need only think of adventure games in text mode (Zork, 1977), specifically linked to the presence of keyboards, these being more practical for verbal interactions, or "points and clicks" games designed for use with a mouse. The main

29 - Human-Computer Interaction, a discipline of computer science that deals with the designing of new interfaces.

subject of this book being joypads, we have left this whole area to one side, although certainly it cannot be overlooked in the general story of the video game, if only because some pad makers have included keypads in their models!

Lastly, these early video game features show how most interfaces are inherited from existing technologies. And then the joypad swept the board as the must-have solution, offering a relevant, integrated engineering synthesis.

Since its defining feature is its pad form, we come now to the evolution of the shape of video game peripherals—from the basic box to the joypad, we shall see how the engineering principles that we have just described are organized in a hand-held device.

Part 2 - Gripping

A joypad's silhouette is a part of its makeup. Its overall shape is instantly recognizable, from the original brick, which was gradually streamlined so as to fit more comfortably in the user's hands. This chapter will describe these advances by showing how gripping, the ability to hold an object with the whole hand, has played a key role in the development of joypads.

The previous chapter presented buttons, joysticks and switches, the basic engineering principles brought together in a box providing "remote control" of a game on a TV screen. In this section, we shall look at the influence that users have had on the arrival and evolution of the joypad.

The joypad as a remote control box

Spacewar! and Tennis for Two showed us how the early embodiments of the joypad in the shape of a small remote control box were present from the very beginnings of video games. Back then, the main idea was to have a dedicated peripheral to control appliances not designed for games such as oscilloscopes and computers. However, following these two laboratory prototypes, the very first "proper" video games did not keep these rudimentary boxes, since with their integrated design with monitor and interface, within a terminal, arcade games had no need for such a "remote control".

The advent of video games into people's living-rooms pushed designers towards the remote control idea. With this novel gaming console hardware, the television screen became the core feature. Now this choice involved various constraints. The major issue was to do with the fact that the buttons on the actual set could not be used for play; first, this would have placed the user far too close to the screen, which would have caused eye strain. And secondly, the television interfaces were neither convenient nor suitable for controlling the games then available: they were not designed to do that[30]. The buttons or knobs had been designed for one-off interactions such as switching channels or adjusting sound and picture quality. In addition, designers in those days also realized that to operate television controls so fast and furiously was liable to damage them in no time. This was not counting the fact that there were so many different models of TV set that no unified model would have been possible. And designing games for each brand of television would have been a costly, lengthy and fastidious process to insure compatibility between appliances.

So it was with the Magnavox and the consoles that followed (Channel F, Atari VCS) that the need was felt to have a proper "remote control", leading to the advent of the game controller, known in French as a manette, a term previously used for mechanical hand levers. Now this introduction of a dedicated interface did not have a smooth ride, as a perusal of the patent filed by Ralph Baer for the forerunner of the Odyssey[31] will show. In that document, the engineer indicated two possible embodiments of the console. One was a block containing both the CPU and the knobs merged into a single appliance. The other, subsequently adopted for all consoles, separated the appliance into a CPU and two individual controls, so as to avoid having the players too close either to the screen or to each other. The presence of these two options in the patent demonstrates how the designers were not sure of themselves or of their design's potential uses.

When gaming arrived on home TV screens, this was a whole new setting that was being colonized: the living-room with the presence of armchairs and sofas and maybe a coffee table or a carpet. This meant that each of these elements had implications with regard to the posture that could be adopted in front of the screen. It is easy to see intuitively how players were not going to play standing up, as they did in front of Atari's Pong (1972) in a café! But the desire to bring arcade games to the home console was so great that the same technical principles were put forward for these game controllers. As we saw in the previous chapter, the

---

30 - One might however imagine games that take advantage of this, but they would be of a very different kind than arcade games!

31 - U.S. patent #RE32282: Television gaming apparatus.

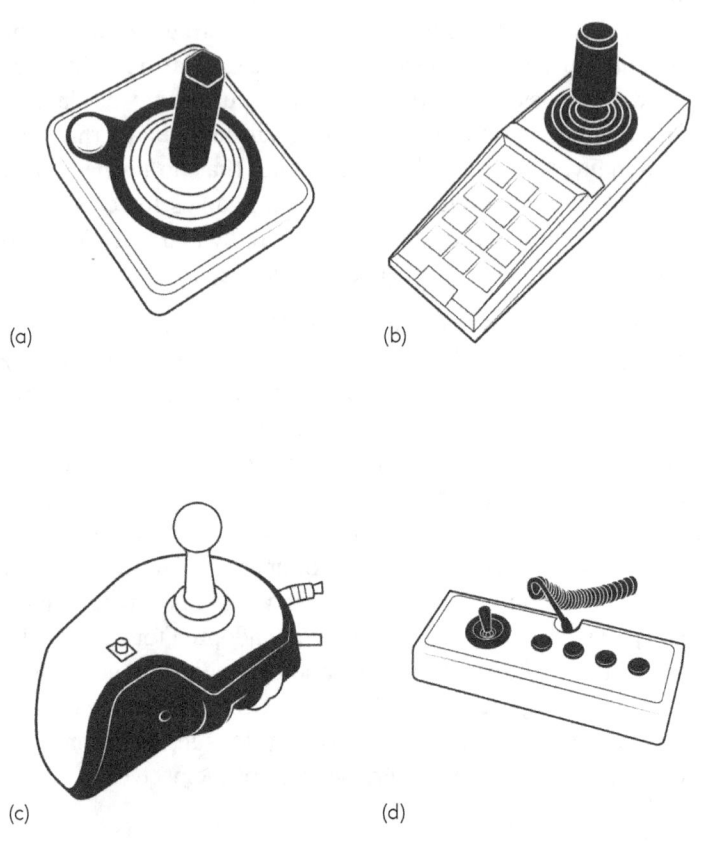

(a)

(b)

(c)

(d)

Figure 12: (a) VCS configuration, (b) Atari 5200 configuration,
(c) Speedking configuration, (d) Vectrex configuration

arcade peripherals were thus directly transposed, with joysticks and paddles featuring on the early game controllers with the Magnavox Odyssey, the countless Pong clones or the Atari VCS.

However, both these types of peripheral had two crucial drawbacks with regard to their grip. First, they lacked versatility in terms of the number of games that they could control: both paddles and joysticks called for one hand to be entirely dedicated to operating these interfaces. And this meant that only the other hand was available to press one or more buttons. This is where the second disadvantage came into play: this second hand was only free if it was not being used to hold the apparatus! This involved being able to put the joystick down on a table to free the other hand, which was generally tired and suffering from cramp. Holding the object in this way was obviously a great inconvenience if players' postures are taken into account, either slouching on their sofas or lying on the floor. In the case of the paddles, what to put the game controller on was not an issue since it had to be handheld in order for the other hand to turn the knob. To put it on a table called for some uncomfortable contortions on the user's part! Given that it could only be operated with both hands, the paddle's lack of versatility became a glaring problem for designers wanting to offer some more complex gameplays than the one-directional movement of simple racquets.

So it was around this time that people began looking for a satisfactory solution to a design issue that might be described as follows: how do you allow a player to control a video game in a varied and sensitive enough way when one hand is looking after the joystick and the other is able both to hold the object and to press the buttons? In answer to this question, a brief review of the evolution of joysticks points to four possible solutions, as shown in Figure 12.

The best known proposition is the VCS, with a central stick and a side button mounted on a more or less tall base. This was Atari's choice for the VCS, and Spectravideo's for its entire Quickshot range (1982), and likewise Kempson's. These models actually came with suction pads to allow them to be mounted very firmly on a support. Such a line was adopted by computer peripheral designers, this device being appropriate in the context of an office desktop. This line survived later on mostly for flight simulators.

Another solution involved the Atari 5200 configuration (1982), already being used by Interton in 1978. This was a game controller with a small overhang at the base of the stick, so that the peripheral could be held like a handle. With this in the left hand, a righthander could use their left thumb to press the buttons while holding the controller... while the right hand was used to work the stick. This solution was reprised by Coleco with their Colecovision

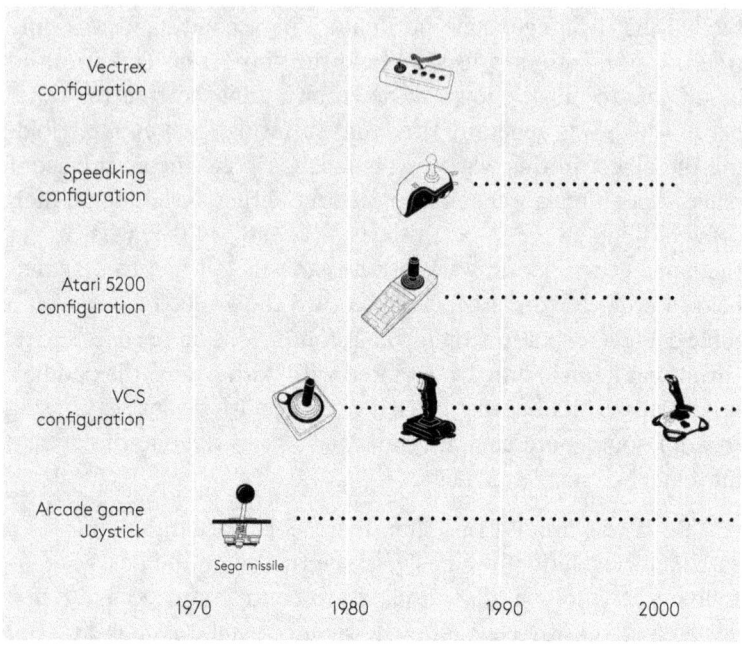

Figure 13: Diagram of joystick evolution by adopted shapes.

in 1982, which offered a smaller joystick. To a lesser extent, it was also Mattel's choice for the Intellivision in 1978, with an ancestor of the D-pad in the shape of a disk instead of a stick. But this line did not last long in the history of interfaces. This was because later models held in one hand, like the Wiimote, were designed to be operated by that hand only, leaving the other hand to hold a second device (the nunchuk). There was also a by-product of this setup with the Konix Speedking (1985), offering the possibility of having a base molded to fit snugly in the hand. This solution enabled a stick to be manipulatable with one hand while the other was used both to hold the item and to press one or more buttons placed under the base (and not on the front as with the Atari 5200). This was one potential ancestor of the trigger.

Lastly the Vectrex game controller developed by MB in 1982 provides the last possible type of line: an oblong brick with a small joystick on the left and a set of four buttons. It could be placed on a support, as can be seen from its underside fitted with four mini-pads to stick to the support and hold it down. Oddly enough, the dimensions of this object were not at all thought out in terms of the size of a player's hands, but to match the width of the monitor in which it could be stored. The game controller's consequent width was in fact an excuse for "filling" the object, hence the four buttons on the left!

The overall appearance of this small Vectrex brick is somewhat similar to a joypad, but it was still too wide to be held in the hands and was operated solely with the thumbs. Even though utilization of the joystick (with the left thumb) was more or less practicable, the buttons were too far apart for the right thumb to be able to press them and at the same time hold the controller itself. On the other hand, the Super Famicom or Neo Geo arcade joysticks may be seen as being derived from this solution. Although featured on consoles, they were used exclusively on a table and were reserved for certain converted arcade games.

For all these gamepad lineages, and this can be seen in the photos in video games advertisements of the day, players generally had to go into contortions in their living-room to operate their game controllers. Either the player had a paddle, or he placed his joystick on a support. With hindsight, these different solutions are interesting from the standpoint of how devices evolved, since they evidence the search for the optimal shape, which had to be satisfactory for the human anatomy and be worked with both hands, along with the possibility of offering multiple gameplays requiring more than just a stick/paddle and a button.

The grip is such a complete constraint that for several years all attempts to solve the equation proved unsatisfactory. With the paddles, joysticks and arcade games, the whole hand was used as a mode of interaction to move objects around the screen, with the index fingers pressing the buttons. Joypads were designed as a way of solving these problems with a straightforward solution: offering a brick large enough to place several buttons on it, and small enough to be workable with both hands. This relied on our opposable thumbs, a basic distinctive feature of the human morphology. Having thumbs facing in the opposite direction to the other four fingers makes for prehensile hands that can grasp objects and hold them firmly.

But to explain this, as often in the history of techniques, we need to make a detour[32]; notably because this solution comes from a parallel lineage to the early consoles and arcade games: that of portable electronic games, with the beginnings in the field of a Japanese firm which we have not mentioned so far: Nintendo.

Thumb-operated mini-games

A historic manufacturer of card games and later toys, the Nintendo company was substantially overhauled in the late seventies, with the launch of a research unit working on a gaming range called Game & Watch. This vast collection of small portable electronic games, produced between 1980 and 1994, was constructed with the impetus coming mostly from Gunpei Yokoi. The designer of numerous successful toys and the head of Nintendo research and development unit 1 (R&D1), this engineer was the mainspring of several great finds that we shall come back to.

Following on from many other innovators and long before "user-centered-design" became fashionable, it was while observing his peers that Yokoi had the intuition that took him to this field of the portable game[33]. Indeed, observing Japanese tilting train commuters having fun with liquid crystal calculators on the local high speed train (Shinkansen), he noted the enjoyment that these people were getting out of having a miniature appliance to play with to kill time.

As in the case of Ralph Baer with his idea for a console to operate with a TV set, Yokoi had to put the idea on the back burner... until one day he was given a chance to talk it over with the Nintendo boss, Hiroshi Yamauchi. This was a complete stroke of luck, as Yamauchi's limousine was a lefthand drive and Yokoi was the only person able to drive this sort of vehicle when the chauffeur was off sick.

Requisitioned to take the Nintendo CEO to one of their partners who manufactured Sharp liquLCD monitors, Yokoi was

---

32 - On the notion of the detour in the evolution of engineered objects, see Wiebe Bijker, Of Bicycles, Bakelites and Bulbs: Toward a Theory of Sociotechnical Change, MIT Press, 1995.

33 - Florent Gorges, L'histoire de Nintendo 1980-1991, l'étonnante invention: les Game & Watch, Editions Pix'n Love, 2009.

able to tell him about the projects that were running through his head, including one to create miniature games intended for adults. This idea did not fall on deaf ears, and not long afterwards, Sharp dispatched a representative to Nintendo to do a project feasibility study. So Yokoi and his colleagues got down to work on the project.

So far, there was no great surprise; Nintendo continued down a path that others were also exploring. Mattel, in the United States, had also launched a line of portable mini-games starting in 1976, tapping into the same interest that pocket calculators had generated. As the then marketing director, Michael Katz, emphasizes: *"It was the mid '70s – a time when Pocket calculators were a new product and were getting smaller and less expensive. Everyone had to have a little handheld calculator. I said to Richard Manning, Mattel's director of preliminary design: 'Can you design a new type of games that uses LED technology similar to that in a calculator but that could be portable, battery powered and the size of a handheld calculator? He went away and came back with the prototype of the first handheld game.[34]"* This was Auto Race, which came out in 1977, a game in which the user had to avoid obstacles represented by LEDs which lit up intermittently.

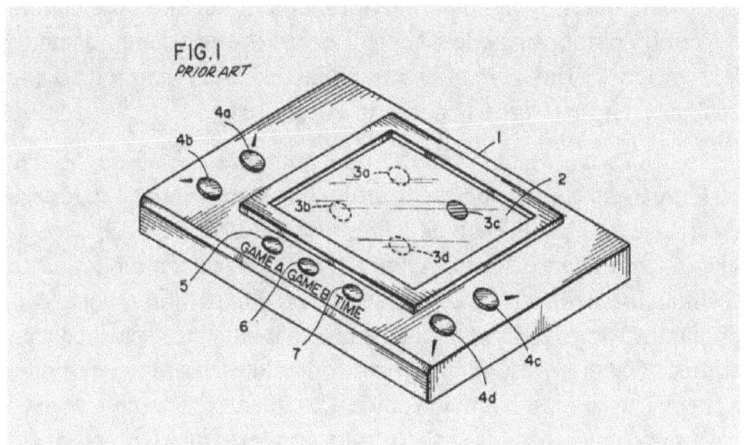

Figure 14: The appearance of a Game & Watch, according to the patent for the directional pad

34 - Cited in Tristan Donovan, op cit.

In Japan, Yokoi's team adopted a different approach. Through greater depth of understanding of the background of the potential users in whom they were interested, they developed a different interface from Mattel's. After studying public transport users closely, they soon realized that the key thing about the objects they wanted to design was their size. As Gunpei Yokoi stressed: *"For an adult, using a big toy in the Shinkansen is extremely embarrassing. How could we design something that can allow people to play with, without being frowned upon by people in the vicinity? While seating, we generally keep our hands tight on our laps. I realized this was the ideal position to have fun without attracting attention. However, with our hands crossed, the only way to interact is by using the two free thumbs. An horizontal design quickly appeared as the best solution. The shape of the Game & Watch was thus though mostly to allow adult to play secretly ! [...] It was then possible to have fun only by pressing on a limited number on buttons.[35]"*

With such a bundle of constraints, the small pack format fitted with a screen and operated with buttons pressed by both thumbs struck the design team as being the most obvious solution. Indeed, it is highly likely that the oblong shape of the LCD screen and the electronic board lying underneath it actually dictated the Games & Watch's parallelepipedal shape. Also, back then there was much less variety to the ways of creating plastic molds than today, and such basic forms were the norm for cheap items.

Given Yokoi and his team's target audience, they used the size of a business card holder as a tardstick. With this template, the electronic game was seen as being discreet enough to be acceptable to its intended users. After all sorts of incidents relating to technical issues and the overall cost of the apparatus, these "Microgames" were released under a name that has since achieved icon status, "Game & Watch". They had worldwide sales in the millions, a timely success for Nintendo since it enabled the Japanese firm to earn some much-needed cash after its previous flops with products like the Chiritory toy vacuum cleaner.

As regards the interface, these ancestors of the portable

35 - Takefumi Makino, **Gunpei Yokoi: vie et philosophie du dieu des jouets Nintendo**, Editions Pix'n Love, 2011 (Our translation).

console were initially equipped with a limited number of buttons. The first model, "Ball", which came out in April 1980, had two action buttons (move left/move right) and another three to select various game modes or the time (hence the "Watch"). Over time, the front gradually changed, with the addition of more buttons and an extra screen and later the advent of the directional pad, to which we shall return in Part 3. The need for something small, which was very present to begin with, was quickly dropped given the great success of these games among children, who took to this item much more readily than adults did.

From the Game & Watch to the first joypad

While the Game & Watch games are interesting in themselves, what we are also interested in here is their subsequent influence on Nintendo console peripherals. When in the early 1980s the company's executives decided to launch the home appliance for plugging into a TV set, the interface for these electronic games was to prove to be a crucial source of inspiration.

Nintendo soon came to the same conclusion that Atari had reached: the potential market for multi-games consoles playable on a TV seemed to be a bright prospect. So in 1981, whoever was in charge at the time contacted Masayuki Uemura, head of Nintendo's second research and development unit R&D2, and set out for him the following target: *"He said the next thing would be video games for play on home television sets and asked if my department would develop them. [...] Yamauchi-san made various stipulations. He said the games wouldn't be built-in, but rather we would adopt the cartridge system, which was just then becoming mainstream. What's more, he told me to make a machine that wouldn't have any competitors for three years.[36]"* And the Nintendo chairman gave him eighteen months to achieve that target: designing the future Famicom console.

With this impetus from his line managers, and the pressure coming from the R&D1 unit, which was going from strength to strength with the Game & Watch, Uemura and his staff at R&D2 got down to work. The technical pitfalls with respect to the hardware and its programming were in proportion to the ambitious targets set[37]. Among the questions addressed in the design stage, the choice of game peripheral proved crucial. Despite Nintendo's experience in games for TV, their earlier projects merely offered a dedicated interface for each game, to be plugged into the TV. With the principle of a multi-game console on the other hand, a new constraint appeared: the control accessory had to be flexible enough! Uemera and his teams realized that what was required was to create an interface capable of controlling several games with complex gaming mechanisms, and the console had to be upgradeable as well (since his bosses wanted it to last three years at least). He summed up the design parameters as follows: *"One of our most important issue for the development of the Famicom was the controller. At Nintendo, we had the experience of arcade games and Game & Watch. In both cases, it was possible to look at the screen while keeping the control interface in the field of vision. But here, the box was far from the television and we were wondering about the shape that should be used so that players avoid staring at it while playing.[38]"*

For Uemura and his colleagues, the existing interfaces did not look satisfactory. To use a keyboard soon appeared over-complicated, especially for a console intended for playing games and not for performing calculations or editing documents. Also, owing to financial considerations, they were able to eliminate some other options fairly quickly; the use of joysticks seemed a natural choice, but was ruled out on account of the excessively high cost of signing license agreements on the American patents. The Nintendo management wanted to keep the console price at rock bottom, and did not want to pay a license fee to the joystick patent holders. The cultural factor also appears to explain this rejection of sticks, since Japanese home interiors are different from their western counterparts, not so spacious and with different furniture. Uemura realized that the control peripheral was generally going to

37 - For a detailed history, see Florent Gorges, 2011, op. cit.

38 - Ichiro Utsumi, **Nintendo. Gulliver Shôhô no Himitsu**, Nihon Bugeisham Tokyo, 1991 Cited in Florent Gorges, op. cit. (Our translation)

be lying around on the tatami or under the coffee table. For him, chances were that someone would end up stepping or sitting on it, which could cause either personal injury or break the joystick. So the need to find an alternative to these existing peripherals was an inducement to look elsewhere.

At the R&D1 office, the Game & Watch line and the recent model created for the Donkey Kong game in 1982 offered a cheap and sufficiently user-friendly solution: the Famicom game controller might be based on electronic game controllers! So much so that Takao Sawano, a renegade employee with R&D2, suggested to Uemera the idea of adapting this type of interface for the console project. Although some of his staff were not convinced, Uemura offered to have Gunpei Yokoi lend a hand with the future Famicom game controller. Accordingly, the interface was overhauled, most notably the screen was done away with, being considered surplus to requirements, as the players would be watching the television. As Uemura recounts, the result soon met with approval: *"Our first attempts were fruitful. Games could be controlled without any problems, without putting much tensions in the wrists, or forcing us to look at our moves.[39]"*

In short, this brief history highlights the "circulation" of one type of interface from one area (portable games) to another (console games). This transposition is a common mechanism in processes of innovation, as shown by the reuse of aircraft joysticks for gaming, or (leaving video games) the conversion of the typewriter into the personal computer keyboard.

A quick glance at the Game & Watch series evidences the legacy of these electronic games that the joypad came into. The rectangular shape and the positioning of the directional pad and buttons are a natural example of this. Given this ancestor, it is fascinating to see this parentage between the joypad and an item designed to be discreet, the size of a business card and resembling a pocket calculator with its tiny screen. These then are the constraints that led to the brick format. This choice heralded the start of a line of rectangular game controllers, with pad models for the early SEGA consoles (SJ-150, SJ-152, Master System control pad), the game controller for the NES (the west's version of the Famicom) (produced by the head designer at Nintendo of America Lance Barr, the NEC consoles (PC Engine, PC Engine Duo, Super-Grafx), the Amstrad GX-4000 or the even more massive Commodore CD-TV.

In those days, the game industry competitor that SEGA was, innovating with the launch of the first arcade joysticks, was content to follow the Nintendo joypad. Unfortunately, owing to the lack of documentation, there is little more to be discovered about this stage. We may however hypothesize that SEGA, seeking to outdo Nintendo in terms of their machine's technical capacities, sought to be more innovative on the hardware side than on the interface *per se*. The shape of the Famicom joypad having become a standard in view of the console's impressive sales figures, it seemed more relevant to follow this benchmark model.

With the rectangular form, frantic use of the buttons began to become widespread; so much so that doctors coined the word *"nintendonitis"* to describe the pains and cramp felt by players using it for too long at a time. Holding a small pad in the hands and pressing on it in such an intense manner led to the need to modify the ergonomics of its design. The first to try and improve it were not the manufacturers, but certain third party developers keen to latch onto this flourishing bandwagon. In this way, during the 1980s, some pads might be wrapped in a rubber protection, giving a better grip on the pad so that the buttons could be pressed faster. The Power Grip model brought out by Dynasound for the NES was designed with this in mind. This type of enhancement brings us to the next stage, which involves changes to the actual shape, more in line with the way the human hand grasps things.

Towards more developed ergonomics

In the late 1980s, with mass production of video games consoles, hardware manufacturers soon felt an urgent need to differentiate between their products. To achieve this goal, both the hardware and the actual games came in for transformation.

Nonetheless, there was some fierce competition among the manu-facturers of game controllers as well, most notably with respect to their shape, when the designers of these peripherals observed a need to have boxes that were more suitable for intensive gaming sessions.

With the NES's next generation of consoles, the first develop-ment strategy involved making the most of new plastic molding techniques in order to offer rounded edges to fit snugly in the palm of the user's hand. At SEGA, this meant a larger joypad taking the shape of a mask, with the Mega Drive. The game controller was curved as if each side of the brick had been twisted downwards.

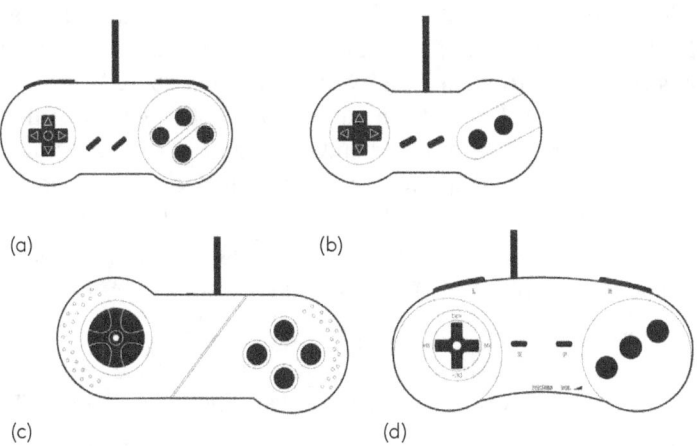

Figure 15: (a) Super Nintendo joypad, (b) NES-039 joypad, (c) Joypad Gravis gamepad, (d) 3DO joypad!

This distortion made the peripheral easier to grasp, but the sharp angles on the foot of the pad were sometimes found to be painful after playing for some time. Nintendo also became aware of the need to offer a new game controller designed to deal with "ninten-donitis". With the "Max" model for the NES, which was brought out for a limited audience in 1988, the curved mask solution was considered, with two bulges underneath to block the fingers. In the line of this type of curved joypad, we also find the Mega Drive 6 button controller (1993), the PC-FX by NEC (1994) and the SEGA Saturn pad (1996). But this solution was gradually abandoned.

For the new Nintendo console in 1990, a second approach was chosen, with the dog bone metaphor. The Super Famicom and rereleased NES[40] pads in 1993 adopted this silhouette comprising two circles positioned at either end of the pad, with the directional pad on one of them, and the buttons on the other – and this, like bone-shaped toys for dogs. Each of these spherical ends made it easy to hold in the hands, without the problem of the sharp base on the Mega Drive joypad. While the Super Famicom joypad was fitted with two incomplete circles (the curve of the circle being present on the base only), this was not the case with the NES-039 model, which with its two visible circles was very close to the bone shape. Meanwhile, the Gravis (PC Gamepad in 1993) and the CD-i 910[41] pads from the European brand Philips in 1998 adopted an unusual silhouette: as on the Super Famicom, the circles were not full circles, but the position of the rounded part was different on either end of the pad. Such an offer meant that the pad could be handled equally comfortably by left-handers as well as by right-handers, simply by rotating it through a hundred and eighty degrees, with the buttons becoming the directional pad and vice versa.

Despite this ergonomically rather well thought-out format, this type of joypad did not last. Interestingly though, Panasonic adopted a halfway solution in 1993 with the 3DO console. This involved taking on the appearance at once of the curved mask and two circles at each end of the pad. This approach is evidence of the possibilities for hybridizing different pad forms.

This dog bone format is also a silhouette that we find among the first prototypes of the Sony PlayStation gamepad. Maybe this was due to that brand's collaboration with Nintendo during the project's early days. But it was the mask-shaped pad with the SEGA Mega Drive that served as the starting point... giving rise to the successive game controllers of the Dual Shock PlayStation, which have since become an unshakable standard with their handles.

In this regard, the history of Sony game controllers and their

40 - Called NES-101, NES 2, Top Loading Model or Top Loader.
41 - It was in fact the same model as the Gravis, only in a gray color to match the CD-i.

shape, making a break with earlier models, is interesting in terms of the creative processes that brought it about, notably because it shows a cultural exception in a Japanese management style somewhat averse to personal initiative. Up until the late 1980s, the brand, whose core business was in electronics for the general public, restricted its involvement in video games to producing electronic components and sound boards for other consoles, including the Super Famicom. Ken Kutaragi, the engineer in charge of these projects, was then one of the architects of the closer collaboration with Nintendo in the early 1990s for a "Play Station" project that failed to materialize, a hybrid of that console with a CD-ROM player that was carried by the two brands. When this effort was abandoned, Kutaragi continued working on an independent project for the gaming device that was to become the Sony PlayStation released in 1994.

The design of this prototype then fell into the hands of Teiyu Goto, manager of the Sony Corporate Design Center. Goto had been given carte blanche to design the different elements, console, game controllers and memory cards. While his initial proposals for the CPU received instant approval from his line manager, Kutaragi, he had a harder time selling his game controllers! As he recalls, "I have worked at Sony for twenty-one years now, but there has never before been such a difficult product. The controller was considerably harder to design than the console [...] The console itself was a relatively easy design process, but we went through a great number of stages with the controller.[42]"

The first time Ken Kutaragi set eyes on the pad prototypes that Teiyu Goto had spent over a year designing, he rejected them in no uncertain terms: *what's this? The shape is original but it doesn't look very easy to use.[43]* Kutaragi was negative especially because the proposed form did not conform to the standard model that he had in mind, namely rectangular with flat rounded corners as on the Super Famicom.

---

42 - Reiji Asakura, Revolutionaries at Sony, McGraw Hill, 2000.

43 - Ibid.

Goto's novel design took a completely different line; the pad was arranged around two handles that resembled horns added onto the bottom of a standard gamepad. To design this type of game controller, Teiyu Goto had prototyped a number of models with several different lengths of grip in a block of acrylic foam. He found this shape interesting because the two extensions meant that the hands took up less space around where players were pressing the buttons. The designer had of course noticed how the Super Famicom joypads needed to be held tightly, as the hand was not fully in contact with the pad's lower support. So, adding on grips, he felt, was a solution to holding the peripheral naturally while getting a good grip on the bottom part: *"you just support it from underneath with your fingers. Moreover, because there's a gap between the controller body and the fingers, even when you're engrossed in a game, perspiration doesn't accumulate. It evaporates away.[44]"*

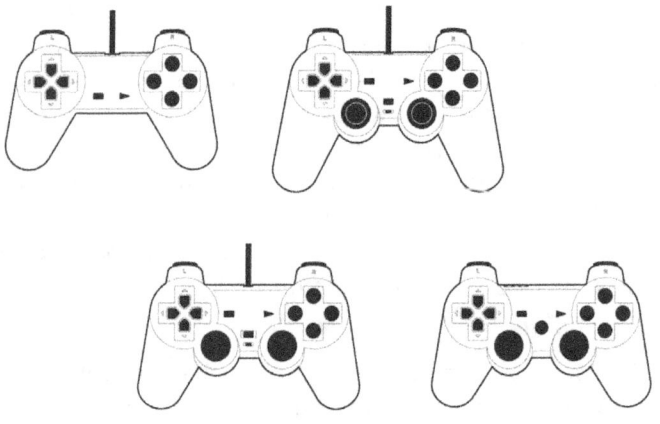

Figure 16: dual shock, dual analog, dual shock 2, dual shock 3

To test this hypothesis, Goto tested his game controllers with a group of children who played Super Famicom on a regular basis. This confrontation with unpracticed users successfully demonstrated how easily they took to the grips. By watching these young players, he also realized that they were using the pad rather differently from what he had been expecting. The children seemed freer in their movements, and could raise, turn or lower the pad without being as restricted as with a flat joypad. This possibility of having such a loose grip on the controller encouraged Goto to see it as being a relevant solution.

Unfazed by his boss's very negative reaction to this model, Goto decided to show his gamepad to the Sony chairman, Norio Ōga. Ōga was generally highly critical of early prototypes, but promptly approved this model, finding it very much in phase with the brand image. Unfortunately, he was the only one who felt that way, and the members of the PlayStation team did not like its shape, too radically different from conventional game controllers, and hence liable to be offputting for potential players.

Although Ken Kutaragi and his colleagues had been aiming at developing a revolutionary machine in terms of technology and graphics, they felt the need to have a standard peripheral with which players would already be familiar. Goto sums it up, *"The Super Nintendo was a huge hit at the time, and naturally we wanted SNES gamers to upgrade to our system [...] That's why the management department didn't want the controller to be a radical departure - they said it had to be a standard type of design, or gamers wouldn't accept it [...] They told me that the grip design was simply no good, that gamers wouldn't like it. We did wind up switching to a flatter controller design, and that survived all the way to the point where it was time to start making molds. Just around then, though, we had a 'creative report,' an internal presentation where assorted groups showed their current in-progress work to the top brass. During that report I showed off the flat controller design, explaining that this is how game consoles work right now, and Ohga was totally livid at me. 'This is no good! Change it! What was wrong with what you showed me earlier?' It was a huge boost for me, him saying that in front of everybody -- it made me feel like I had it right all along.*[45]*"*

For Teiyu Goto, a truly cutting-edge machine really deserved to have an unusual controller. In the end it was the Sony boss, Norio Ōga, who came down in favor of the grip model: *"As far as*

45 - Reiji Asakura, op. cit.

I can see, this grip-style controlled is very easy to use, something that children and adults alike would enjoy using. Stop arguing and adopt this design! [...] I'm the president, so you must do as I say. Otherwise you're all fired." Thus the designer's viewpoint, during his time at Sony, seemed to be highly respected. As Goto recalls: *"I still clearly remember him saying that 'the control stick is the most important part of any game [...] Ohga flies airplanes and helicopters, so he used the term 'control stick' to talk about the controller. He really liked the grips on the controller because it let him get a 3D-style grasp on the situation."*

So it was thanks to this support from above that Goto's handles won out against the Sony PlayStation joypads. The grips on the bottom of the PlayStation pad heralded the advent of a new "wing grip" line, as it was called by observers of the field, likening these side attachments to a bird's wings. We shall now see how this family of joypads became the majority among later models.

The evolution of the wing grip

The different joypads for Sony's PlayStation consoles were all designed following the same principle: the Dual Analog with its extra two analog sticks (April 1997), the Dual shock (November 1997) with smaller grips after the Japanese complained that they found them too long, the Dual shock 2 (March 2000), the Sixaxis (November 2006), the Dual shock 3 (November 2007). While there were few changes between 1997 and 2006, with the PS3 game controller model some subtle modifications started to appear. As Goto, still a designer with Sony in 2006, reports: "We also modified the shape at the point where the middle fingers support the controller. Before then, there was a pocket to ensure that middle fingers would fit tightly. For the new controller, we shifted the grip toward the front and made it shallower to increase space for the middle fingers. It is a small change, but it gave the middle fingers enough space to move back and forth, allowing users to grip the controller more freely. Also, we made the rear of the controller more curvilinear so that it will better fit the middle finger joints. Thus, the controller can be held within a wider area. When you hold it, you can immediately feel this difference. We improved the shape of the area where the middle finger supports the controller, so that supporting fingers are more comfortable when pushing buttons. These changes are extremely small but they make a big difference if you play games for a long time.[46]"

The constancy of the uniform design of the Dual Shock pads over three generations of consoles is a rare enough occurrence for us to pause over it. With the possible exception of the Microsoft X-Box pads, no other game controller has seen such continuity. Having said that, such an approach on Sony's part indicates not so much a desire to carry on regardless as responding to the need not to disturb players who had adopted this model as a de facto standard. Because too radical a step can always backfire!

In this connection, when the Sony designers wanted to change the shape with the new PS3, in 2005, there was such an outcry that the designers promptly reverted to the standard model with handles! It was a brief episode, nothing more than the presentation of a prototype at the flagship Electronic Entertainment Expo E3, in June 2005. The pad was boomerang-shaped, the main section of the controller and the extended grips forming an integrated semi-circular unit. This was a shape little used throughout the history of game controllers, with only Apple and their Japanese partner Bandai giving it a try, in 1995, with the AppleJack (Pippin). Following the success of the first two PlayStation models, Ken Kutaragi, by then the chairman of Sony, was looking for a more radical innovation for the third version of the console. For the brand, the E3 expo was seen as a venue where this avant-garde model could be unveiled to the industry and to the media, and any criticism could be fielded as well. And this is what ultimately happened. In actual fact, the feedback was so negative that the design team had to backpedal. Goto offers the following explanation: "It was very futuristic visually, but practically speaking you only had to hold it to realize how it compared to the Dual Shock 2. You know there are so many players who are used to the PlayStation controller; it's like a car steering wheel and it's not easy to change people's habits [...] Also PS2 and PS3 provide backwards compatibility; the

46 - Interview with Teyiu Goto: http://www.playstation.com

ergonomics should be the same when you play games from the previous generation but without having to bring out the 'wired' controllers. It is for these reasons that we reverted to the shape of the
classic controller.[47]" This special case provides us with an instance
of a recurring problem with the ergonomics of these interfaces:
once users have become accustomed to a given mode of interaction, they have great trouble changing their habits. This is known
as path dependency: users are as it were on a path or in a rut that
they cannot leave out of habit. This is a common occurrence in the
history of engineered articles. The QWERTY computer keyboard,
a throwback from the old ribbon typewriter, is another example of
this. We are so used to it that it is hard for us to find the time to
learn any other arrangement of the keys!

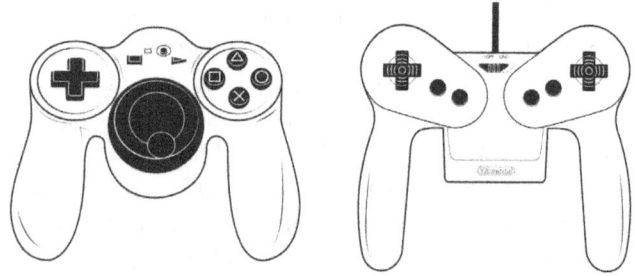

Figure 17: Jogcon (NAMCO) and Virtual Boy (Nintendo) game controllers

While Sony set the tone with the handled game controllers,
other players in the video games industry gradually came round
to the idea – but not necessarily by copying the PlayStation model
in every detail. Nintendo, as always, tried to innovate on the basis
of this wing grip design. The first attempt only reached a tiny audience since it was the above-mentioned Virtual Boy, released in
1995 and designed by Gunpei Yokoi. With under a million sales,
this model for Nintendo was a resounding flop. The console came
in the shape of a "virtual reality" headset resting on a two-legged
support designed to be set on a table. The apparatus simulated
a 3D perspective effect with red light emitting diodes produc-

ing monochromatic graphics[48]. With such a setup, the marketed games promised a stereoscopic view of the gameplay area. Unfortunately, the result was not all that it was cracked up to be, with very average graphic quality and a rather uncomfortable playing posture (you had to lean with your elbows on a table)[49]. And yet, the Virtual Boy gamepad design had several innovative features. While the major change to this peripheral lay in the two D-pads, this was the first Nintendo joypad to have handles. An ergonomic feature on them was the notches on the underside for the fingers. This M-shaped model had two of the longest "horns" seen in the entire history of gamepads. This meant it could be effectively held with the hands, leaving the thumbs free to press the buttons.

Compared with the brand's previous experiments, the highly symmetrical unit was fairly large in size. The silhouette closely resembling a human pelvic bone appeared again with Namco's Jogcon

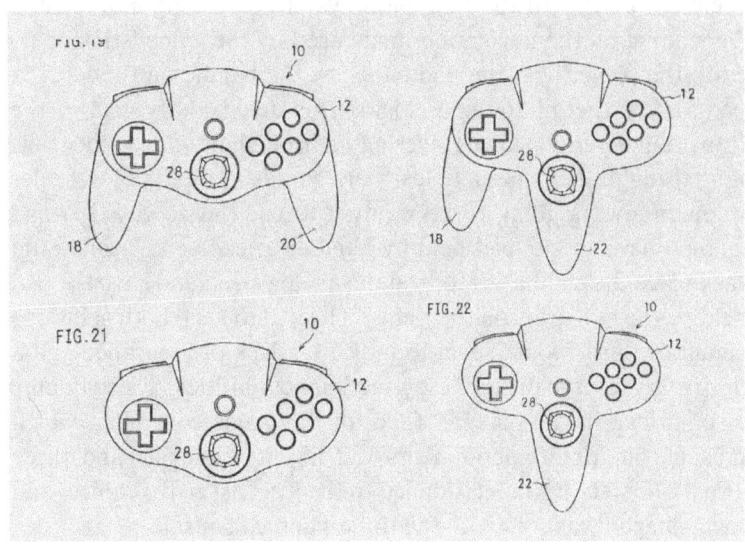

Figure 18: Forms of the Nintendo 64 game controller based on the presence of the analog stick in the center, as described in the patent filed by the Nintendo engineers.

48 - Owing to LEDs of this color being so cheap and using so little energy.

49 - For further details about this failure, see the dialog between Iwata and Myiamoto on the subject: http://iwataasks.nintendo.com

joypad, which was also M-shaped with a large knob in the middle with which to simulate a steering wheel in car racing games. Fascinatingly, the N64, designed during the same period and released a year later (1996), also used this base... to offer a trident version of it, i.e. with three handles! The Jogcon might therefore be seen as an intermediate stage between the Virtual Boy and the N64 game controllers.

With the last-named, it was obviously not a matter of using each part of the trident all at once, but rather of offering several different ways of holding the pad depending on the game being played: either by holding the two end grips, or by holding the center handle along with the one on the left or the one on the right.

As we shall see in the next chapter, this gamepad marked the return of the analog stick, after an absence of several years, in addition to the D-pad. Now the multiple ways of holding the joypad seems to be due to the multiple ways of controlling movements. Depending on the navigation mode used by the game (stick or D-pad), the player held the pad either by the handle on the left (D-pad), or by the middle one (stick). This duality is typical of the transitional periods in engineering paths; it shows the doubts running through the Nintendo designers' minds at the time: were developers always going to be wanting to use the good old D-pad (and so have the joypad held by handles at each end)? Or would they place the emphasis more on the analog stick (and have the pad held by the two grips on the right)? The will to keep both solutions simultaneously would seem to indicate a lack of assurance and a desire to preserve different interaction possibilities. These doubts also surface in the patent[50] filed for this game controller, which presents multiple embodiments varying between one and three grips. This relative indecision led to the least assertive choice, and the gamepad was sold with the three-handled console.

The upside-down trident shape of the N64 game controller unfortunately had a disturbing effect on some players. They were seldom sure of the configuration to be used to begin with: should they be holding the middle handle? Or the one on the right? Or

---

50 - U.S. patent #5984785: Operating device with analog joystick.

the one on the left? Over fifteen years later, on retro-gaming forums the jury is still out as to whether this pad is any good! Hence
this trident look is only to be found on the early prototypes of
the 3DO joypads and after that no other maker took the risk. As
Kenichiro Ashida, in charge of designing the controller, reminds
us, "The Nintendo 64 controller was designed explicitly with the
American market in mind, and perhaps that was a mistake. It was
too large for most children in Japan and they had to make a sacri-
fice because of it. I wanted the GameCube controller to reflect the
universal ease of the Super Famicom, that's why it's been changed
so many times. I wanted a natural correlation of the buttons on
the face of the controller, while keeping it small enough for everyone.[51]" So we may consider this model to have been a one-off line
in an evolution that is now extinct. Taking advantage of his experience with this controversial form, Kenichiro Ashida then did away

Figure 19: Xbox and Xbox S game controllers

with the long horns on the Virtual Boy and the trident format on
the N64. He did this by offering a GameCube[52] pad very much in
phase with the "wing grip" line following on from Sony in terms of
the grip. Later on, the joypad model designed for the Wii, the Wii
Classic Pro, also carried on this line as an addition to the Wiimote
and the nunchuk.

---

51 - http://spong.com/article/2195/A-day-in-the-life-of-the-Nintendo-hardware-designer-
Its-a-tough-job-but-someones-got-to-do-it

52 - The DOL-003 model, DOL for "Dolphin", the codename for the GameCube project.

In a somewhat different style, the designers at Microsoft, who joined the console market in 2001, also opted to fit in with this line with a two-handled pad[53]. This choice saw the "wing grip" established as a standard for newcomers to video game hardware design. Actually, the first model (the "Duke") designed by Horace Luke and sold with the console when it first came out, was particularly bulky, so wide in fact that some players could not reach the D-pad because it was too far away from the analog stick! What happened was that when the hand was placed on the handle on the left, the thumb would be naturally positioned above the stick. To move it to the D-pad meant moving the hand along the grip, which is particularly inefficient from an ergonomic viewpoint.

Some observers moreover theorized that this game controller had been designed for American users with bigger hands! This was the reason put out by Microsoft when the S (for small) version of their joypad was released, designed by Alan Han for the Japanese market[54]. The model in question was such a success outside of Japan that it was used as a template for the joypad's second version, which was then sold along with the console.

Staying with the double-handled solution, the Xbox 360 game controller released in 2005 and designed by John Ikeda came with a joypad that was basically very similar to this second Xbox controller. The pad had the same grip, but it had a more regular, nonfragmented shell. One last point on this particular lineage, the Wii U Classic Pro joypad model released in the fall of 2012 for the Wii U console in fact reverts to an overall appearance very similar to that of the Xbox 360 game controller.

This wing grip line now stands as the standard for joypads. The predominance of the two handles from the three major console makers (Sony, Microsoft and Nintendo) would seem to indicate that this interface has settled down. This is notably because both players and developers have gotten used to this optimum format that allows a maximum number of buttons to be placed on the front of the pad.

53 - Dean Takahashi, D. Opening the Xbox: Inside Microsoft's Plan to Unleash an Entertainment Revolution, Prima Press, 2002.

54 - Official Xbox Magazine, No. 11, October 2002.

Alternative lineages

Obviously the above description is restricted to the main joy-pad lineage that we still find to this day. Thus we have moved on from the oblong brick to the rounded mask, later followed by the advent of the handles. Now despite this straight-line trajectory, we should not overlook other paths explored by console and game peripheral manufacturers.

Since the Wing Grip is the commonest model around, it is interesting to look at the variations on this type. The pad on the Amiga CD-32 console produced by Commodore (1993) and the Intel Wireless Game Pad (1999) are two models that offer handles pointed upwards and not towards the base of the pad, in a U-shape. The type of shape is no more than a footnote as it was adopted by no other game controller.

More commonplace, one of the alternatives that keep cropping up in the history of joypads is the one-piece circular pad. These pads are produced by Micom Soft with its XE1-AP (1990), Atari with the Jaguar pad (1993), the 3D controller on the SEGA Saturn (1994) or the Dreamcast (1998), the first X-Box from Microsoft (2001) and the N64 released exclusively for the Chinese market in the iQue range (2003). In this line, discontinued after 2003, the general principle involved having a massive peripheral with a surface broad enough to add on extra buttons. This round or nearly round appearance was gradually altered with the addition of small grips on the bottom of the unit, or even sunk into the underside, starting with the SEGA Saturn. So this shape reminds us of a cross between the wing grip model and the compact unit type. The main complaint that emerged from the owners of these models came from the pad's overall lack of balance, because for players, an effective game controller has a surface area large enough to leave gaps between the buttons, but small enough to be held comfortably in the hands.

When this surface area becomes too big, the object becomes awkward to hold and the richness of interaction you get with the large number of buttons is not enough to offset this drawback. For failing to strike this balance, these large models were gradually abandoned. It is nonetheless interesting to note how at the time of the preliminary research prior to designing the Wiimote, a project for a rounded game controller was mooted. Called "cheddar cheese" by the development team, it was a kind of orange disk on which there was a large star-shaped button in the middle, surrounded by three buttons and with accelerometers included inside. Long story short: "Nobody liked it"[55], Miyamoto says. So much so that it fell by the wayside.

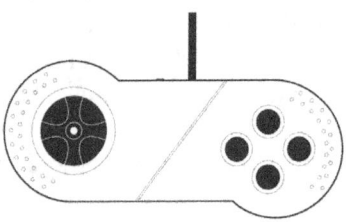

Figure 20: CD-i game controllers

Alongside the line of wing grip game controllers, and present from the earliest consoles, we again find joypads with single-handed operation. Seldom used in the history of the video game, this type of peripheral took on a shape broadly resembling the television remote control. It was notably Philips who adopted this solution with the release of the CD-i in 1990. The Dutch company was a television manufacturer at the time and was looking to innovate in this sector by offering a product that would be more than just a gaming console but an audiovisual and educational device as well. On account of this lineage, and this aim, the CD-i controller then was devised as a fairly standard rectangular remote control with an analog ministick that could be operated with the thumb of the hand holding the object. This type of pad is basically fairly similar to the early Atari 5200 type joysticks we were talking about earlier, in the sense that the shape and grip are similar. The difference lay in the fact that the joystick was so small that it could be manipulated with the hand holding the pad (rather than the other hand).

55 - Osamu Inoue, Nintendo Magic: Winning The Video Game Wars, Vertical, 2010.

The designers at Philips went on to design models still usable with one hand and that look better ergonomically, but with no stick, and then two pad models: a standard one with a "dog bone" format (going back to a model from the Gravis brand), the other in the curved mask shape. As these projects led to no further developments, the one-handed peripheral format was discontinued for a time. Only a few models by third party makers, like those of the ASCII brand ("one-handed controller" and "grip") subsequently moved in that direction. However it was Nintendo with its Wiimote in 2007 who reverted to this one-handed interface designed like a remote control.

And in this case, the reasons for this return are worth looking at more closely.

The various game controllers on the Nintendo consoles show their designers' dogged determination to innovate and try out new paths. With the Wii, which was codenamed Revolution, there was an even greater determination to differentiate from other brands.

The thinking that went on prior to designing the Wii was different than for the earlier models. In light of the fierce competition between Sony and Microsoft over graphic quality and the types of game likely to attract highly skilled players, Nintendo opted for an alternative strategy. Their designers realized how, in addition to the existing audience, here was an opportunity to design a more affordable console in terms of the interfaces and titles on offer. The idea was to convince a huge untapped market: the broader, more family-oriented market of non-players.

Hence it was literally the aim of making it easier to "come to grips" with the game controller that became the starting point. As described by Kenichiro Ashida, in charge of designing the gamepad, the Nintendo staff themselves felt the need to make the device less complex: "I think it was when the overall concept of Wii began to emerge. I personally felt that the GameCube controller was the culmination of all controllers that had come before it, and that it couldn't be improved via the traditional concept of simply adding to it. More than anything else, I felt as though the controller and I were incompatible. Having a family, the time I had to play hard games decreased, and a gap between my 'creator self' and my 'player self' was born. When I then came to understand the Wii concept, I felt strongly that this would be a console that I too could enjoy.[56]" The design team then saw the relevance of the operating principle of motion sensors with accelerometers: "More specifically, I felt that it might be time to reconsider the entire gameplay style of grasping the controller with two hands, sitting glued to the TV until morning. Of course, I'm not rejecting that intense style of play, but I did feel that taking the whole idea of grasping the controller with two hands back to the drawing board offered a glimpse of the future.[57]"

But choosing this kind of technology implied choosing an interface that could be understood and accessed by players unfamiliar with the world of video games. Although his fellow game designer Shigeru Miyamoto wanted a stick-shaped unit, the design team initially went with a joypad held in both hands. The group soon realized the problem with this solution: pointing at the screen with the middle of the pad would have been too unusual for users. In this way Genyo Takeda, the head of development for the Wii, came round to the idea for a pad held in one hand. Myiamoto then realized the value of something shaped rather like a cell phone or the remote on his car satnav: the way these devices look is self-explanatory. This is why the single-handed device was selected.

This is how the Wiimote came into being, with the name as a portmanteau word made by the combination of name of the console and the term "remote". As Satoru Iwata, the Nintendo CEO puts it: "The TV remote in your house is something that always sits within reach and is picked up and used by everyone all the time. Since I wanted the controller to be used in the same way, and since it ended up looking like one in the end, I strongly believed that it should be called a remote. And also because one of the most fundamental questions behind Wii's development was why some people use the TV remote all the time, but hesitate to pick up a game controller. So I really insisted that it be called a remote[58]."

56 - Interview given to Video Games Blogger in May 2007.
57 - Ibid.
58 - Interview in the "Iwata Asks" series.

Despite the reference to the remote as giving the pad its over-all shape, it remains in the line of the early joypads, for when you turn a Wiimote onto its side, you revert to a Famicom or NES pad as the D-pad and the two side buttons are still present. Smaller, and with fewer buttons than the TV remote, this peripheral required all the Nintendo designers' ingenuity, marking a break with the past yet in continuity with it.

For all that, unlike earlier models such as the Philips CD-i, the way of controlling the Wii console did not boil down to just a long object held in one hand. Indeed, a remote control pad as simple as the Wiimote could not be suitable for all types of game (notably for first person firing games), for emulating earlier games, or to be backward compatible with GameCube games. That is why the Ashida team resorted to turning the Wiimote into a mini-controller and to combining several peripherals together, and offering an additional item: the nunchuk.

As Kenichiro Ashida describes: "I first heard about the idea for the Nunchuk from Takeda-san. He said, 'can you try to make something like this?' There were also requests from the development teams for Metroid and other software titles asking for a new kind of controller that uses both hands, that can offer a new type of gameplay. And so, yet again, we started out by molding another clay model. At first, I also considered a design similar to that of the remote. But since it was so obvious that the right and left hands are used differently, I realized that making the designs similar would just make it harder to control. When I asked for Mr Takeda's advice, he reassured me that it was fine for them to be different since they would be used separately.[59]" This was also the solution that Sony came up with for their PlayStation Move in late 2010, with a "motion controller" and a "navigation controller". While the former part is used to detect user movements and the manipulation of four buttons, the latter comes with the conventional Sony buttons, X, O, L1 and L2, an analog stick and a D-pad. So it is interesting to note how the ideal of the basic, single-handed peripheral soon faded away behind the need to have elements to add onto it.

59 - Ibid.

Whether it be the Wii or PlayStation Move, the shape to be chosen depended on both the desire to provide a gestural interface (requiring fewer buttons) and the need to hold onto enough complexity to be able to play more standard games. As it was not easy to strike this balance, you had two types of model coexisting: those with accelerometers (Wii, Move), and the more standard models in the "grip" line: the Dual Shock 3 for the PS3 and the Wii Classic and Wii Classic Pro pads for the Nintendo.

We need to remember however that this is not the first time in the history of game controllers that we have seen this kind of proposition. For the Mega Drive in 1988, SEGA had built a prototype game controller in two elements operated independently, one by each hand. The hardware manufacturer Hori had also released a joypad for PlayStations 1 and 2, which could be unhooked around the center axis and split into two separate parts. It is also interesting to mention the NegCon model from Namco (1985), which may be seen as a halfway solution between a standard pad and a two-block game controller. By allowing the two ends of the pad to rotate around a central axis, this joypad enriched the gameplay without any extra buttons. That is what was offered by this peripheral mostly used in racing car games. Lastly, before Microsoft joined the console production business, the Seattle brand was producing game controllers for PC games. One of them, the "SideWinder Dual Strike", released in 1999, also followed NegCon's lead by offering rotation around a central axis, which was connected to a potentiometer so as to detect bending movements performed on the controller and thereby add an extra control method to certain games.

The last alternative line to the wing grip game controller, the rectangular brick and direct descendant of the Famicom pad, is a possibility seldom encountered, but currently on its way back. In 1991, Commodore, the maker of the Amiga computer for the general public, designed a multimedia home device, the CDTV (standing for "Commodore Dynamic Total Vision"). The game controller on this product was also designed as a multi-function remote control. The brick format is the one that was then adopted: a fairly broad rectangular pad with a large number of buttons. More recently, Nintendo's Wii U (2012) also reverted to this parallelepipedal format with the Gamepad, which is composed of a touch screen around which various interfacing elements are arranged (analog sticks, D-pad, buttons etc.). This shape seems in this case to have been dictated by the presence of the built-in rectangular screen, and not by the ergonomic quality of the brick-shaped game controllers.

Marginal lineages

Along with the aforementioned lineages, many other forms can be found as well. These are generally not the handiwork of the major video game platform brands, namely Nintendo, Atari, SEGA, Sony and Microsoft, but come from third party makers. For there is a whole output being manufactured by other players, accessory specialists, copiers or hackers, and handymen working in their garages. So it is worth taking a look at these lesser known models and examine some minority cases. Although they are only a sideshow, they do reveal some interesting aspects of the video game culture.

If we look at game controller models with strange, exotic shapes, the first alteration that is immediately obvious is to do with personification. As video game worlds developed, their population of heroes and creatures gradually turned into fully-fledged icons; so much so that some popped out of the game itself to lend

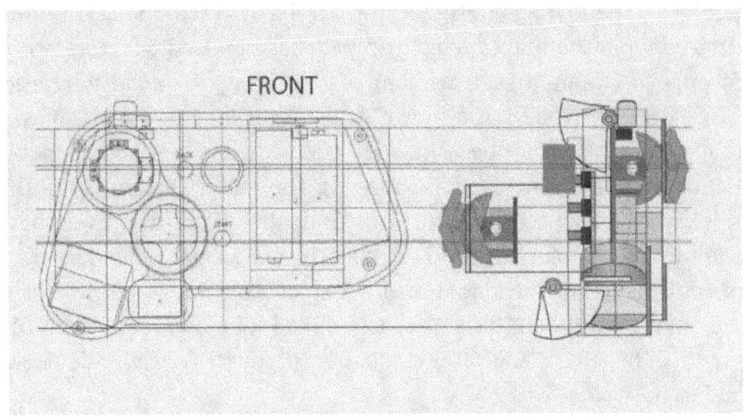

Figure 21: Game controller designed for hemiplegic players (Ben Heck)

their shape to the game controller. A good example of this is the "Slime" pad, which takes the shape of one of the monsters in the game Dragon Quest, since it is a blue-colored inverted teardrop the base of which is made up of a directional pad, two analog sticks and buttons similar to the conventional PlayStation pad that inspired it. With such a device, a balance was struck between a functional easy-to-hold surface for the player, and the creature's visual identity. This personification thus established a direct correspondence between a character on the screen, which happened to be an enemy, and the object held in the hands. But this type of proposition remained a one-off in gamepad evolution.

Then it is only a short step from personification to personalization. Players were in fact customizing their pads without waiting for their brands to give them the wherewithal. The Web is awash with sites describing how to dismantle and alter game controllers in this way. Such transformations mostly affect the buttons, but you sometimes find alterations being made to the shape. Most instances of customized pads involve the choice of colors or transformations to the molding of the pad shell.

However, the most interesting cases concern players with special needs, notably due to some handicap. We may think in particular of the joypads designed for one-handed manipulation, but derived from the line of wing grip pads (as opposed to the remote form). An example such as that of the "Single-handed wireless Xbox 360 controller" produced by the designer Ben Heck, shows that such an aim can be achieved. The principle behind this particular instance, involved positioning the pad elements on both sides, with a single-grip shape. Customization like this proves that a minimal form can be found to bring together a maximum number of controls on two surfaces (on either side). The non-standard placing of some of the buttons of course called for a certain amount of practice, but the change shows just how deft users of these devices had to be!

Above and beyond customization, there is another possible, albeit more prosaic, way of modifying a gamepad; this involved integrating the peripheral within another type of object or merging

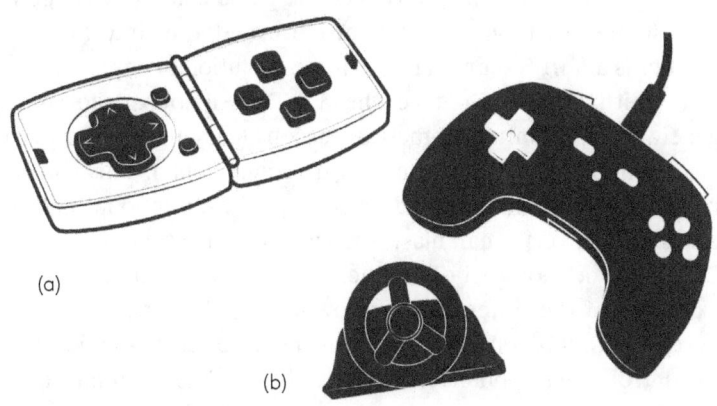

(a)

(b)

Figure 22: (a) foldable GoPad Atari, (b) M.A.D. USB

them together. A classic example of this is the steering-wheel into which a Wiimote can be inserted. We may also mention the game controllers on the GameCube and PlayStation 2 shaped like a chainsaw, and produced in a limited series by NubyTech for the game Resident Evil 4 (2005). In this example, the proposed transformation is esthetic rather than functional, the idea being to plunge into the game world, and not to enrich the gameplay through novel interactions on the pad. The pad in question was none other than a Dual Shock inserted in a plastic shell made to look like a chainsaw. From a more functional standpoint, there are a number of game controller-cum-computer mouse hybrids.

This item can be used in two different ways: a mouse set on a support, or turned over like a joypad with a fairly similar shape to the Wii Classic. But these game controllers are no more than a footnote here.

In addition, the advent of virtual reality technologies in the eighties also saw a number of projects for interactive gloves or force feedback systems. The one offered by Mattel for NES, the "Power Glove" (1989), was among the first commercial products of this type, but also a resounding flop. With this kind of approach, we are obviously moving away from the idea of the joypad, since the pad as an object disappears into another interface.

Finally, one last adaptation of the game controller shape lies in its miniaturization from standard forms. Making interfaces ever smaller is a fairly common trend in the evolution of engineered objects. With the Atari GoPad or the M.A.D. USB, joypads follow this general rule, mainly for practical reasons (easy to transport), and also technological reasons (miniature components). This category includes folding mini-joypads made up of a directional pad and four buttons, very small mask-shaped pads, or sets of buttons and D-pads to be mounted on a touch screen with suction pads. The existence of these items shows how joypads have become an important standard since they are transposed as they stand in order to control other appliances such as tablets. This is an interesting phenomenon because the idea then becomes adding buttons onto an interface that is not supposed to need them!

Gradual standardization toward a single model

Starting from the original oblong shape, we may distinguish between six main lineages in the evolution of game controller shapes: the brick, the curved mask, the two-handled "wing grip", the dog bone, the rounded model and the one-handed remote control format. Obviously this is a very cut-and-dried classification, and some intermediate items need to be placed between these categories: the three-handled model (midway between the remote control and the rounded model), or the boomerang (midway between the mask and the wing grip).

These different families pictured in Figure 22 did not necessarily have a continuous, long-lasting existence. Thus some of them have fallen by the wayside: the brick and the dog bone models were discontinued in the early nineties, while the rounded/semicircular type was no more than a brief episode between 1993 and 2003, etc.[60] So in the late 2000s, the lines that lived on were chiefly the "wing grip" and the remote control models. The latter, in the case of the Wii and Sony Move, is no more than a joypad split into two parts. Strictly from the evolutionary standpoint, we

---

60 - In this regard, the completely spherical SEGA Saturn pad is a fine example of a one-off appearance followed by extinction.

note stabilization toward a virtually single form. This therefore appears to be what players and developers consider to be an optimum standard. Here we summarize the elements described in this chapter explaining the path towards stabilization.

In the first instance, manufacturers passed through a diversification stage, when each sought to stand apart from the others while working from a common basis. The box started out being rectangular, on account of the technical constraints, i.e. the plastic shell molds offered little variety and overall they were designed to house electronic boards which were themselves rectangular. The first players then realized that the shape was not ideal and that there was a problem of morphology; players would complain of getting cramp, and so the designers understood that the brick shape was not very easy to grip. Hence curves were gradually added to the unit to make it fit the hands. Meanwhile, advances in plastic materials and the shape of the molds in design and industrial production also helped along this trend towards gentler, less angular shapes.

In addition, the increasing power of processors, graphic boards and memory chips has revitalized the creative possibilities. Faced with the increasing complexity of the game world, game designers have opted to add on buttons to give players the benefit of these engineering enhancements. This has led to an increase in the pad's surface area and a search for solutions to make it comfortable to hold, while freeing up the thumbs to press the buttons. The advent of the "wing grip" format was seen by players as so ideal that it became a standard. This break saw game controller evolution move on to a second stage, in which competing makers converged towards a common form that users found satisfactory. Sony and Microsoft adopted this approach with their rather similar-looking joypads. Note also how the recent arrival of game controllers in two sections such as the Sony Move or the Wiimote-Nunchuk pair reproduces these two stages over a shorter time span.

Also, the wing grip shape has become so commonplace that it has become a model for control interfaces. Think for instance of engineering objects outside of the field of video games that have been directly influenced by joypads. This is the case with the Sony

The shape of the first controller - a small brick - was developed on the Game&Watch model.

The research for a more ergonomical grip, the development of 3D interfaces and the addition of action buttons contributed to the differenciation of shapes.

Geometrical shapes are added to the basic brick, giving it a "dog bone" silhouette.

The Wii U comes back to the original shape.

2012

1991

1990

1987

1987

1985

1985

1984

1983

1993

1988

1993

1990

1990

1988

1995

1990

1993

2006

The controller loses its symmetry and is splitted in two.

1994

2010

With a 90° rotation, the basic shape becomes a one hand controller.

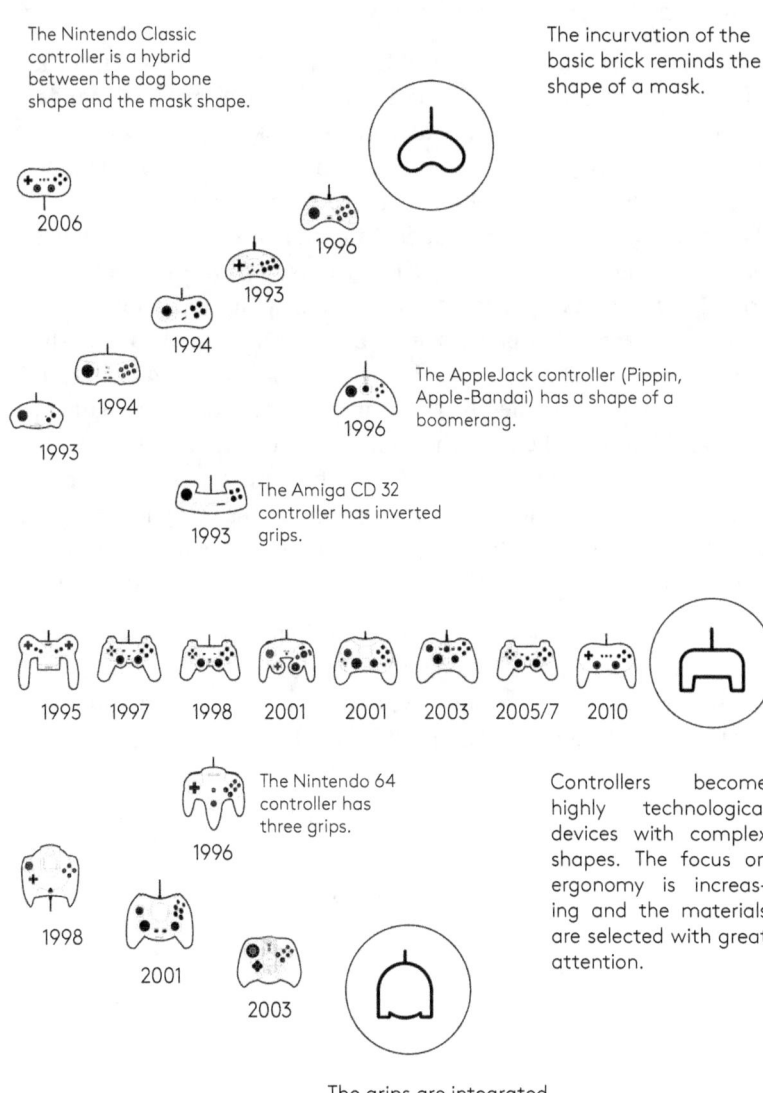

The Nintendo Classic controller is a hybrid between the dog bone shape and the mask shape.

The incurvation of the basic brick reminds the shape of a mask.

2006

1996

1993

1994

1996

The AppleJack controller (Pippin, Apple-Bandai) has a shape of a boomerang.

1994

1993

The Amiga CD 32 controller has inverted grips.

1993

1995   1997   1998   2001   2001   2003   2005/7   2010

The Nintendo 64 controller has three grips.

1996

Controllers become highly technological devices with complex shapes. The focus on ergonomy is increasing and the materials are selected with great attention.

1998

2001

2003

The grips are integrated in the controller shape. The surface displaying the buttons is increasing considerably.

RM1000BP, a remote control for a video camera. It has a shape with two handles for holding with the thumbs which control two potentiometers and various buttons.

With the benefit of hindsight, this chapter shows us how the history of these forms evidences a need to free players' hands. Before the joypad became widespread, back in the days of the VCS, configuring a joystick called for the presence of one hand to hold the controller and the other to operate the knob or joystick. The invention of the joypad made it possible no longer to have one hand dedicated exclusively to the base as both are used at once to hold and to manipulate the pad. Then, with the advent of the N64 and PlayStation pads, something else happened to free the hands; the hand changed from being a gripping mechanism to different functions provided by three areas: the inside of the palm of the hands to hold the pad, the thumbs to activate the interfacing elements on the surface, and the other fingers to activate the buttons on the edge or underside of the joypad. This setup meant that a minimum amount of force was required to activate the buttons with the thumbs, since the rest of the hand was brought into play.

To sum up, we may stress how the grip played a key role in the evolution of the shape of joypads, and this by taking account two features of our hand morphology: opposable thumbs, and allocating functions to the different parts of the hand.

Part 3 - Navigation

The two previous chapters addressed the role of the technical and physical parameters in game controller evolution. Such an analysis should not however make us overlook another very basic element: the video games, and more specifically, what game designers want to get players to do, have also had an effect on the pads themselves.

For while the existence of game controllers can be put down partly to the available technologies and the way we hold things in our hands, the interactions offered in the games have also influenced pad designers' choices.

As we shall see in this chapter, this influence can be seen especially in how characters and objects are moved around the screen. Gaming peripheral designers were indeed forced to imagine various utilizations of the joypad to control movements within the gaming area. From the direction pad to motion sensors to analog sticks, these interfaces have gradually changed over time, and this chapter retraces their evolution.

The advent of the direction pad

In the course of video game history, moving characters and objects around the screen has always been central to creative designs. From the ball in Pong (1972), to the rides in Grand Theft Auto (1997), from the brick in Arkanoïd (1986), to Lara Croft's movements in Tomb Raider (1996), moving around a digitized space has always been an integral part of the video game experience; so much so that the design of the game world and the associated interactions or challenges were often the starting point for many projects. The fact that games should be called things like Spacewar (1961), Space Invaders (1978), Dragon's Lair (1983) or, later on, Super Mario Land (1989) or World of Warcraft (2004), using words with a spatial connotation (Space, Lair, Land, World) shows just how important this component really is.

While nowadays there is a profession called "level design" dedicated to planning the game space in the overall video game design chain, that was not the case when the early computer games were created. These early designers, who were very often just programmers or electronicians, had to take care of a whole string of operations that were later taken over by various people with specific job descriptions. However, this did not stop them from defining what players were going to be able to do, and how they might move around the screen.

We have already seen in previous chapters the multiple interaction principles enabling users to play. Buttons, knobs, sticks and switches were all used for various functions, including navigating within the space of the game. We have seen how these elements were mobilized and diverted to control avatars and objects. But so far we have not mentioned a critical moment in joypad evolution: the advent of the direction pad, an interface dedicated to movements and which has remained to this day a major component of video games peripherals.

To examine the detail of the advent of the direction pad on console joypads, here again we need to make a detour via electronic games, as we did in the previous chapter. Indeed this interface was designed for certain models in the Game & Watch range, and not on a console.

Produced from 1980, under the direction of the R&D1 research and development unit headed by Gunpei Yokoi, these electronic games were a huge success for the Nintendo corporation. The games came in the form of a small rectangular box fitted with one or two screens and a few push buttons. These were used to manipulate the movements of the character appearing on a liquid crystal screen. Up till then, interactions had been fairly straightforward: a ball to catch, objects to avoid, a goal to reach before racing back to the point of departure. Given the controls in the shape of buttons, the gameplay involved either a spatial navigation dimension (moving along the screen), or having a character perform gestures while motionless but able to change posture or shape (e.g. to catch balls thrown up in the air).

For all the designers' inventiveness, it soon proved necessary to complexify the control interface[61], initially through the addition of an extra screen with which to extend the playing area. Later on, Nintendo's then boss, Hiroshi Yamauchi, asked Yokoi and his team to devise games in which players could perform two actions simultaneously. As Gunpei Yokoi stresses, recalling those days: "I realized it became truly complicated. In order to make sens, the actions had to be linked with each other while being distinct at the same time.[62]"

One game in particular crystallized this requirement: Donkey Kong (1981). In it, Jumpman, the character on the screen, had to rescue a damsel in distress, kidnapped by an angry ape, by climbing ladders and avoiding barrels thrown down by the ape. This gameplay involved a further degree of complexity since you had to control the character in all four directions of the plane and make him move forward and jump as well. To make this possible, several solutions presented themselves to the R&D1 teams.

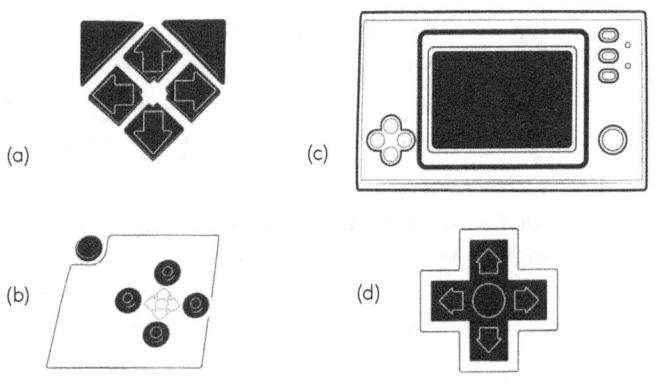

(a) (c) (b) (d)

Figure 24: Interfaces that were forerunners of the direction pad: (a) Split Second, (b) Atari Game Brain, (c) Donkey Kong Jr., (d)Famicom direction pad.

61 - Another possible way explored in third party video games now involves exploring complex gaming forms using just one button. Such an approach is clear proof of how the richness of a game does not depend solely on the number of interfacing elements it offers.

62 - Florent Gorges, 2009, **op. cit.**

The first one involved resorting to the interface conventionally used at the time on arcade games and home consoles: the joystick. So the idea was to add a small stick, along with a jump button. Unfortunately, for various reasons, as Florent Gorges mentions in his book on the Game & Watch series, this solution would not work. In the first place, this mini-stick fitted with two screens like a Nintendo DS prevented the apparatus from closing. In addition, the stick was too thin and fragile, hard to fasten onto such a thin base, and hence easily breakable. There was an improved version of this stick with a flexible plastic washer that held it down better onto the apparatus. Despite its functional quality, this solution gave players the impression of manipulating a nipple[63].

Breaking the joystick down into four direction buttons was also an option taken by the R&D team as shown in Figure 19. One Game & Watch released later even adopted this solution: Donkey Kong Jr. (1982) combined four push buttons that were smaller than on the earlier models. This solution, a forerunner of the direction pad, was also used for other earlier electronic games such as Split Second (Parker brothers, 1980), Select a game from Entex (1981), the Atari Game Brain console (1977) or the game Cosmic Hunter for the Microvision portable console (Mattel, 1981). In each of these cases, there was one button for each direction. These various possibilities, with their different shapes and sizes of buttons, remind us that an innovation seldom occurs just in one place, but is often introduced in several different places at once.

Gunpei Yokoi and his team soon realized that having four small buttons placed in a row was liable to confuse players. To put it another way, in ergonomic terms this was not a satisfactory solution inasmuch as it was hard to tell which of the buttons was to be used. As Takehiro Izushi, the engineer in the then R&D1 team, recalls, *"Mr. Yokoi was very meticulous. He wanted players to have precise control without looking at their fingers. That was why we put a depression in the middle of the d-pad, among other things.[64]"*

63 - Hence the name "Oppai gata kontorolâ" (literally "tit-shaped" controller) as described in Florent Gorges, 2009, op. cit.

64 - "Iwata asks, The Reproduction of 'Ball' for its Thirtieth Anniversary" (2010), in English on the Neogaf forum.

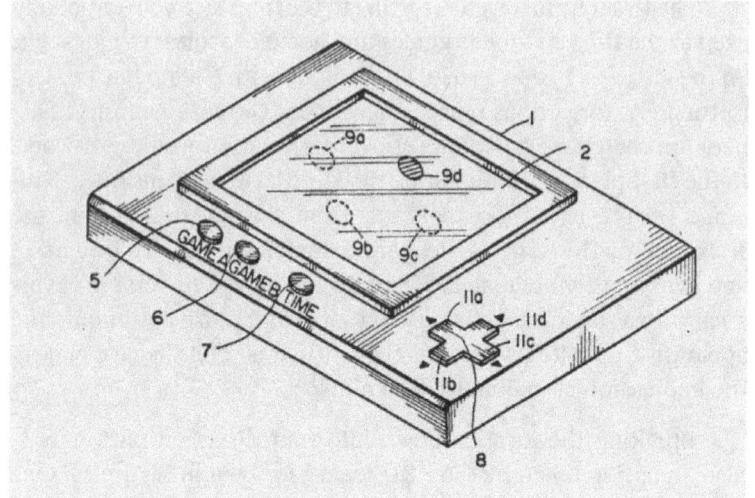

Figure 25: Directional pad as presented in the patent filed by Nintendo.

So coming up with a convincing solution was a fastidious affair. Masao Yamamoto, a designer on the team, describes it this way: *"It took a mountain of trial and error to make that d-pad. We'd give a prototype our engineers had done their very best to refine to Mr. Yokoi for his impressions, asking him 'so? How is it?' He would just say 'it's not ready' That happened over and over.[65]"*

As shown in Figure 19, bringing the four direction buttons together into a single unit proved the key to the problem: the cross they formed meant that there was just one element to manipulate with the hand and you could feel with the thumb which direction was being taken. You only have to try it out to understand: when you press the right arrow, it goes down and raises the left side. In ergonomic terms, sensory information perceived by the surface of the thumb without looking at the interface is known as "proprioceptive feedback". In this connection, the addition of a tiny dip at the intersection of the cross's two axes was another contributory factor, providing a sensory landmark locating the interface center.

Its cross-shape initially earned it the name "cross button" (jyujibotan) by Gunpei Yokoi and Nintendo, where jyuji means [in

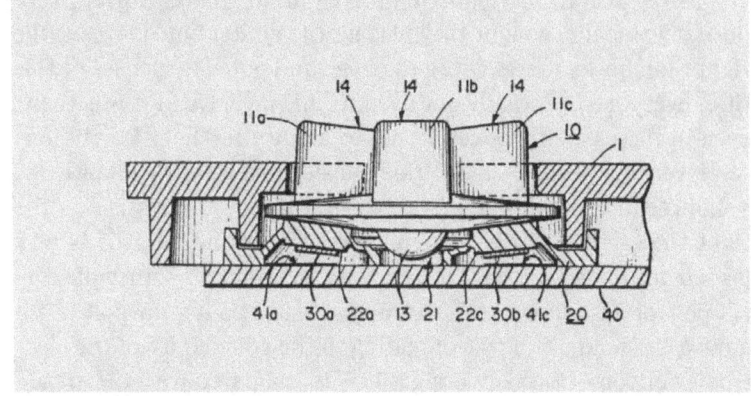

Figure 26: the direction pad seen in profile.

the shape of] the figure ten [i.e. a cross or X], and botan meaning "button", as written in the katakana syllabary often used for transcribing English words. This term later became "jyujiki », where ki is a transcription of "key", until the Americans took to calling it the "directional pad" or "d-pad". In French it is called the "croix de direction" ("directional cross").

The patent on the direction pad filed by Nintendo in 1985[66] also provides further information on this subject. As shown in Figure 25, it is striking to note the presence of the cross on the right-hand side of the Game & Watch. This indeed was the position originally chosen by the R&D1 team. And this is the result of a straightforward presupposition: since movements in the game space require great precision and, given that the majority of the population are right-handed, the design team thought it would be better to position the corresponding interface on the right side. Now history shows that the d-pads were placed on the left. This change may have been due to the "path dependency" phenomenon we encountered earlier in Part 2: users' habits being what they are, sometimes it is necessary to comply with their expectations and the way they do things. With the joysticks on arcade games being on the left to control movements, Yokoi and the rest of his team decided to toe the line rather than confuse players: "in Space Invad-

66 - U.S. patent #4687200: Multi-directional switch.

ers, as the accuracy of shooting was of utmost importance, I suppose developers thought that placing the action button under the right thumb was wiser. Given the huge and populat success of this title, everyone eventually got used to this layout and it was risky, even in the case of Donkey Kong, to modify the habit of millions of players.[67]" But they made this choice somewhat reluctantly, as Yokoi recalls: "I think it's more natural to have a joystick on the right since the majority of people are right-handed. This is why I keep thinking we took an awkward decision.[68]" Other observers put forward more exotic arguments such as a strawpoll taken among the team, or a way of adding to the complexity of the electronic version of Donkey Kong (1981) as compared with the arcade version. It is also interesting to note how peripheral designers had already been wondering about where to place the navigation interface. The designers of the Vectrex pad in fact opted to place the mini-stick on that game controller on the left. As Jay Smith, one of the designers of that console, says: "The placement of the joystick wound up being from a discussion that if you were flying a F-14, or whatever the fighter was at the time, the pilot's hand is in a flight stick on his left, and the throttle in his right. So he does all the flying control with his left hand.[69] "

Moreover, the description of the Nintendo d-pad in the corresponding patent highlights the technical principles behind this innovation. It was a set of components pictured in Figure 21: a four-directional switch, a plate with a set of electrodes on which rests a plastic cross indicating the four directions in an identifiable way through arrows engraved on the surface, a mounting comprising a pivot between the plate, the cross and several pieces of rubber holding it all together.

As we mentioned in the previous chapter, it was thanks to a collaboration between the two entities at Nintendo, R&D1 (in charge of the Game & Watch series) and R&D2 (which developed the Famicom), that the form of the joypads and the direction pads ended up as the interface of the first video game console from Nin-

67 - Takefumi Makino, op. cit.

68 - Florent Gorges, 2009, op. cit.

69 - Retrogamer, Videogames Hardware Handbook: 1977 to 1999, 2009.

tendo. Masayuki Uemura, the head of the Famicom project, not having the funds to purchase licences for joysticks, and finding no satisfactory solution, chose to go back to the cross and adapt it. Some of his team members protested, saying this innovation was inferior to the joystick, which was the standard solution in those days. Soon however, the tests carried out by the R&D2 demonstrated the benefit of the d-pad. The robustness of the device was a major factor, as Uemura states: "The direction cross was far less sensible to shocks than joysticks, and, financially speaking, it was difficult to find a more economic solution.[70] » That is how this engineering principle "circulated" from the world of electronic games to that of the home console, through the in-house research and development teams.

Lastly, we note how this proposed cross-shaped interface differed from another forerunner of the d-pad: the "diskpad" on Mattel's Intellivision console (1979). On this North American console, the peripheral had a small disk providing control in sixteen directions. Back then, the designers of this interface wanted to avoid players having to raise their finger while operating the gamepad. Unfortunately, despite this apparent superiority, not many games required such sensitivity in those days. Also, being so off the beaten track compared with joysticks and paddles, this interface just did not feel right to players.

Copying the model without being found out

The direction pad then quickly went on to become the preferred navigation interface for video gaming. A good way of understanding how this happened involves retracing its evolution while taking into account the large number of copies or references to it, first on electronic games and then on consoles competing with the Nintendo. These were SEGA, Atari, NEC and Namco in the first instance, and later Philips, Gravis, Sony and Microsoft were influenced by Yokoi and his team's design, and made their own adjustments to it.

Figure 27 (page 98) summarizes the different direction pad

70 - Masayuki Uemura, op. cit.

models over the thirty years of its existence. This evolutionary diagram highlights a number of interesting aspects: the existence of several lineages based on distinct forms, some more resilient than others, along with some ever-present d-pad families and one-off modifications that did not find favor with the designers of subsequent models.

Let's first take a look at the broad range of d-pad lines. The standard format of the Nintendo model appears to have remained fairly stable from the 1980s up to the present day[71]. The first alteration came with the SEGA joypads in 1983. On the early models of these (SJ-150, SJ-151 and Master System), the cross was formed out of a square marked with four lines in relief indicating to players the cardinal directions in which to tilt the cross. With Atari, another alternative was found: the insertion of the d-pad inside a circle. This choice was then also taken for the models designed by NEC (from the PC Engine to the PC-FX and also including the PC Engine Duo), Gravis, SEGA (Mega Drive and SEGA Saturn) and Microsoft (the various Xbox pads). This type of d-pad may be seen as a second continuous lineage in d-pad evolution.

The main explanation for this slight modification to the shape of the direction pad is straightforward enough: at the time, the d-pad was protected by a patent[72] filed by Nintendo in 1985 and obtained in 1987. This patent was precisely worded so as to make it extremely restrictive ("The character moving switch is formed in the shape of a cross and is adapted such that characters are selectively displayed responsive to the pressing direction in which the switch is pressed"), thereby insuring the Japanese brand against any copying that might be done by their competitors. Not wanting to purchase a license to gain access to possible utilization of the Nintendo R&D team's invention, the designers at SEGA, Atari and NEC developed models of their own. But obviously they were pretty much carbon copies of the cross designed by Gunpei Yokoi, as it was considered to be an effective standard for controlling movements in video games.

---

71 - Although we may note a reduction in its size from the NES to the GameCube pad.

72 - U.S. patent #4,687,200: Nintendo's multi-directional switch.

These multiple cross shapes thus led to a balance being struck between the choice of a solution similar to Nintendo's, adapted to players' new habits, along with some slight differences to avoid copying too slavishly and picking up a fine. Hence the d-pad is and is not a standard since a single brand owns the patent! Only the SEGA Dreamcast offered a cross that bears a close resemblance to the Nintendo one, but the underlying mechanism was different enough for the makers of Mario and Luigi to avoid being taken to court for patent infringement.

Alongside the standard Nintendo cross and the ones placed inside a circle, alternative shapes and configurations were to follow. These include the exotic cross shapes in Figure 27: the clover leaf on the NEC PC-FX, the cycloid ring on the NES Max[73], the single ring on the Philips CD-i, in anamorphosis on the N64 model released on the Chinese market (iQue), a concave circle for the Apple-Bandai Pippin, etc. For all this diversity, only the cross segmented into four small arrows on the Commodore CDTV, then the generations that followed the Dual Shocks, can be seen as a line that is alive in the sense of continuing up to the present day. In this regard, despite the five year difference between the two projects carried forward by the two makers, it would appear that the two brands came up with the same solution for a fragmented cross, without any deliberate copying on either side.

Several years after the advent of the Nintendo d-pad, it is also interesting to see the repeated presence of mini-joysticks for mounting or screwing directly onto the d-pad. This was the case with the Atari 7800 game controller, the SEGA SG-1000, the SEGA Mark III and even the early models of the SEGA Master System. This determination to combine a previous interface with the cross basically indicates a lack of conviction regarding the proposed choice. This stick-cum-cross was thought up both to avoid putting off seasoned users and to follow the direction taken by newcomers who favored the cross. Once again, it was a matter of striking an ergonomic balance in order to satisfy players' expectations and habits.

---

73 - A cycloid ring that may look like an analog stick but which is in fact a disk that, when moved, presses on the four buttons located underneath.

Another interesting feature is that the changes applied to the direction pad were not always linked to its visual appearance. The underlying mechanics of this interface also came in for some innovations. Think for instance of the complex mechanism of the cross mounted on a small rod in the SEGA Saturn game controller, and most of all the second version of the Xbox 360 joypad in 2010. On this controller, the work of the American designer John Ikeda, the cross could take on either of two different configurations: "Depending on the content you play, you're going to want one or the other. There's no 'This d-pad is right for all things.' Depending on how you use the d-pad, there might be a different d-pad for you. [74]" This was because Ikeda wanted players to have a d-pad shaped like a plus sign, indicating the four cardinal points for precision games like Pac-Man Championship (2010). For fighting games like Street Fighter IV (2009), he found it more effective to have a circular cross in order to perform movements without getting a sore thumb. The adopted solution involved being able to flip the cross over to toggle between modes. Just as the direction pad design is linked to the desire to extend the spatial repertoire in a video game, this change to the Xbox d-pad is another move towards adapting an interface in function of the spatial constraints of the levels present in video games.

Although the d-pad patent expired in 2005, the other brands would seem to be happy with their own models, as they have not reverted to the Nintendo model.

Handling 3D movements with an analog stick

The continued presence of the direction pad on the pads that came after the Famicom is proof of its relevance as the preferred interface for movement. However, after a decade or so, we note a break in the evolution of video game peripherals, with joysticks making a comeback, in a minimal form, being worked with just the thumb.

74 - Everything you want to know about the new Xbox controller: http://www.gameinform-er.com/b/news/archive/2010/11/11/everything-you-want-to-know-about-the-new-xbox-controller.aspx

With advances in electronic components, the quality of the graphics has gradually improved. Both the characters and playing levels have gained extra detail, as more colors, higher definition and more alive textures have become available. These richer gaming environments were slowly built up by searching to replicate reality by taking up visual codes to obtain a resemblance, and in so doing produce greater immersion.

In particular, the addition of perspective during the eighties left its mark on the history of video gaming. The first games offering "three dimensions" resorted to various tricks to give the impression of depth. We may mention for instance pieces of scenery that become increasingly smaller the further they are away from the player (Night Driver, 1976), stereoscopy by sending two different images, one into each eye, and which gave an impression of relief, the representation of mazes with segments of straight lines or ridges which when assembled produce an illusion of depth (Wizardry, 3D Monster Maze, 1981), an "isometric" projection, i.e. a view from above slanted at a 45-degree angle (Zaxxon, 1982), or a scrolling parallax: superimposed visual elements moving at different speeds (Altered Beast, 1988). Later on, realtime generation of scenes and objects in perspective became another predominant mode of 3D representation.

Now in these examples, and into the early nineties, the interface for controlling characters moving in 3D remained unchanged. This was done by pressing the arrow keys on the computer keyboard or for consoles with the direction pad. With them, game designers went as far as they could with possibilities for interaction in order to produce this impression of 3D immersion. For instance, a classic trick used for the Super Famicom games involved giving a third person view (the player sees the object he is controlling) and "sliding" the world continuously in the direction of depth. Star Fox (1993) is the classic example: the direction pad was used for sideways movements, but movement in depth was not really controlled by the player, being a continuous movement determined by the program.

This example shows how the desire to create levels having depth of field came up against the capability of the buttons

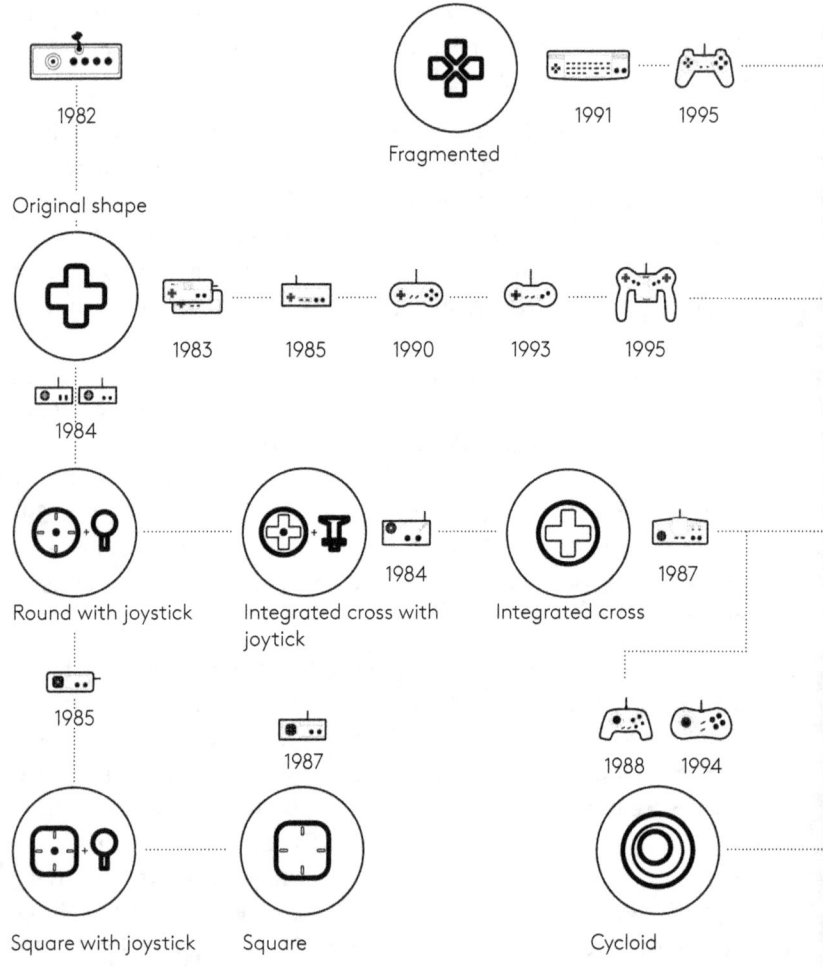

Figure 27: Evolution of the direction pad

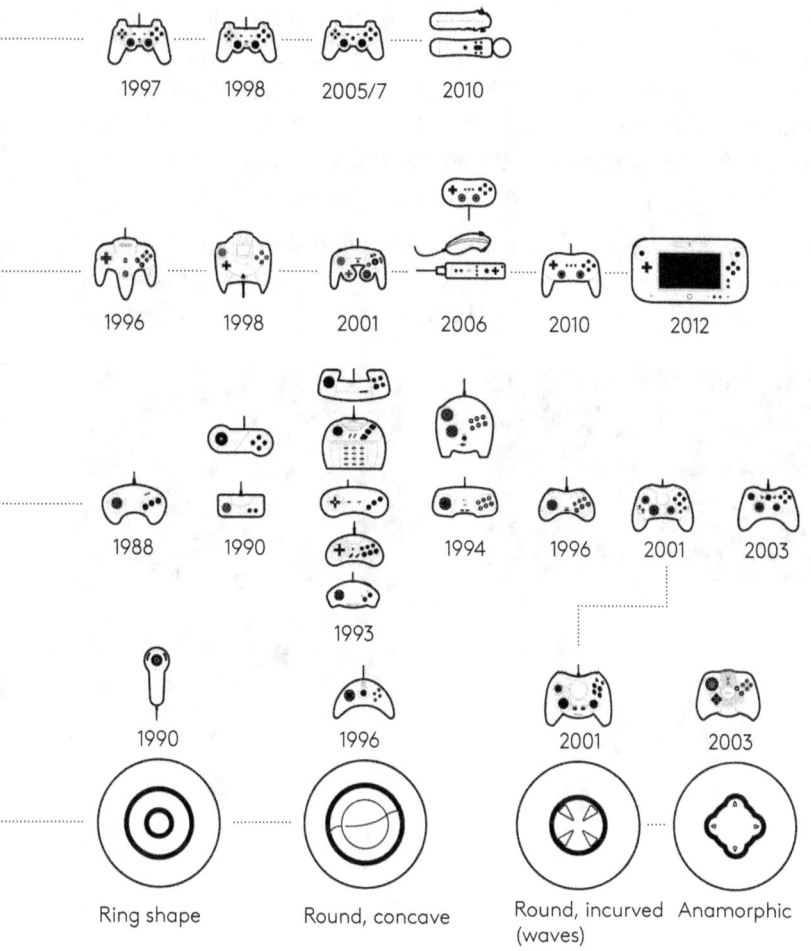

1997   1998   2005/7   2010

1996   1998   2001   2006   2010   2012

1988   1990   1993   1994   1996   2001   2003

1990   1996   2001   2003

Ring shape   Round, concave   Round, incurved (waves)   Anamorphic

and direction pad to make such immersion possible. For all the hardware designers' and software programmers' ingenuity, they soon saw the need to design a navigation interface dedicated to moving around a 3D world. Several different hardware manufacturers have made outstanding contributions to this research. We may think for instance of Mattel and the Power Glove released in 1989 for the NES console. By enabling hand movements to be made with this glove, the idea was to allow players to control an object in the three dimensions of the plane. The reason why this peripheral never really caught on was the lack of precision and the difficulty using gestures and buttons simultaneously.

Meanwhile, the engineers at Nintendo devised the adaptation of the direction for stereoscopic 3D games. On the pad of the Virtual Boy[75] console (1995), the designers quite simply offered to

Figure 28: Various modes of 3D representation: Night Driver (1976), 3D Monster Maze (1981), Zaxxon (1982) and Super Mario 64 (1996).

---

75 - It should also be stressed how this product follows on from some other projects for a 3D interface concerning not the input peripheral (game controller, glove, and mat) but the output device. In this regard, goggles and other virtual reality headsets were used for a long time, with no great success, as a means of representing the digital world.

add on a second d-pad to control these movements in the plane's third dimension. Here again, the attempt ended in commercial failure. However, this was due not so much to the presence of a d-pad on both sides of the game controller as to an accumulation of drawbacks with the device: ergonomically maladjusted, a red monochrome screen that gave people headaches, and an uncomfortable posture for players.

Despite these two flops, Nintendo should not be criticized too much since it was the make that successfully established an interface adapted to navigation in a three-dimensional space. And this was done by reverting to an old device on the N64 console game controller (1996): the analog stick. Let's take a closer look at this revival, which highlights an interesting relationship between game design and hardware interface design.

In the early nineties, despite the phenomenal success of the Famicom/NES, and the rather successful sales figures for the Super Famicom/Super NES, Nintendo soon came under pressure. The economic slump in Japan and the fierce competition from SEGA and later Sony led executives at the Kyoto firm to innovate. To overtake the competition, in early 1993 Nintendo set itself the target of designing an upmarket console with a 64-bit processor and high quality 3D graphics, the whole package to cost under $250.

With this project initially called "Project Reality", then "Ultra 64" and finally, "Nintendo 64", the Kyoto brand was seeking to turn toward what it saw as the major promise of the new generation of consoles: computer generated images or Computer Graphic Imagery (CGI). This was done in conjunction with Silicon Graphics Inc. (SGI), a leading electronics company in the field of CGI technology which designed the processors enabling 3D scenes to be generated in realtime[76].

With this challenge of quality 3D representations in mind, the project focused in the early days very specifically on designing the hardware with which to achieve those aims. Designing the gaming peripherals did not take place until a later stage, so much so that,

---

76 - Silicon Graphics Interview with IGN (1996).

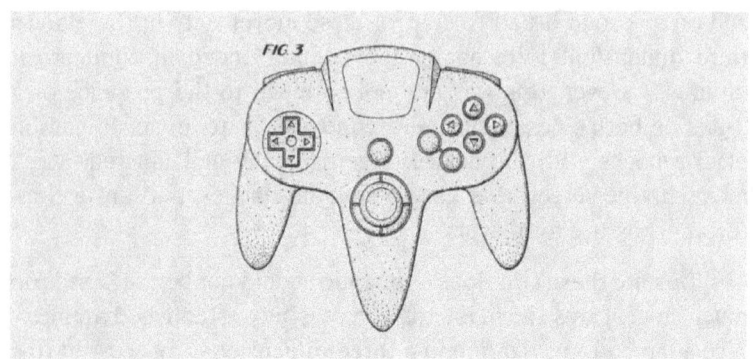

Figure 29: Camera buttons on the joypad (Models and drawings)

for six months, the first games devised for "Project Reality" were tested with modified SEGA game controllers, as Giles Goddard, a developer with Nintendo at the time, recalls: "We had various prototypes – there were lots of them, probably at least 100 proto-types, mostly based around the central stick, how that moved, how well it moved, what shape the thing around it should be – it ended up seven-sided, but we tried many, circles etc.[77]"

Once this hardware test period was completed, under the guidance of Shigeru Miyamoto, Nintendo's game designers began to confront the reality in engineering terms behind their vision of the games that they wanted to create. Owing to the possibility of representing the world in three dimensions, designers wanted to design gameplays in which players could move around the space in every direction. As Myiamoto says, they wanted to "to do a game that recreated an entire world in miniature, like minature trains. When I saw what could be done with 3-D modeling on the Star Fox game, I knew we could do much more.[78]"

What especially caught their full attention was the Super Mario 64 project (1996). The idea was to transpose the 2D Super Mario game platform into a 3D world. Obviously such an aim brought a whole raft of new questions with it: should the player be left free to go wherever he liked? Or should a fixed path be set as in the

77 - Giles Goddard, interview with NGC, 2010.

78 - "The game guys", Nintendo Power Vol. 80, 1996.

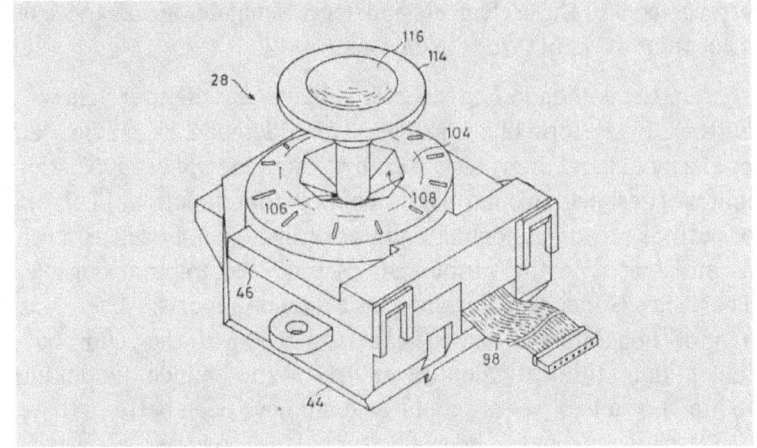

Figure 30: Engineering principle behind the analog stick of the Nintendo 64 game controller as described in the patent.

isometric 3D games? Wishing to enhance this impression of freedom, the game designers opted for the former solution (even though some parts of the game have fixed paths). From the combined work of the hardware and game designers, the choice fell to a pad allowing a compromise to be found for movement with these strictures placed on it. Two complementary arrangements were chosen from among the possible solutions: camera buttons on the one hand, and the analog stick on the other.

The camera control is a crucial element in designing any 3D interface. In a conventional 2D game, the player sees the game world as if it were filmed by a fixed camera mounted perpendicularly in the case of a Super Mario-type platform game, or seen from above in a "shoot them up". But in a 3D world, the game world is as it were filmed by a constantly moving camera. This term designates the given point of view over the portion of the world shown on screen and over the presence of the character to be manipulated (Mario in Super Mario 64, 1996). This is because a 3D representation involves a "scene" that is observable from a certain angle. This angle has to be adjustable so as to show the objects present; they can be superimposed and be hidden behind each other as in the physical environment. So changing this viewpoint lets you see the overall arrangement of these elements and hence simulate the existence of a coherent world in three dimensions[79].

On the Nintendo 64, this role is played by the four yellow C buttons. In the form of a fragmented direction pad, as can be seen on the model and drawings[80] filed by Nintendo in May 1995[81], this unit was designed to control the camera in four directions. This set of buttons proved unpopular and was ultimately not used as much as anticipated in the various games produced for that console. Thus Giles Goddard, a developer at Nintendo reports: "There was a lot of thought about how the camera moved with the yellow buttons – I don't think Miyamoto even liked them. I remember talking to him a couple of years ago, he said it'd have been better to have two D-pads, it would've been a better balance to have the same on the left and right. [82]"

The second key device was the analog stick, which on the other hand played a fundamental role in the history of game controllers. In its case, the aim was to have an interface that could give the impression of continuity in movements through 360 degrees, and not an intermittent interface like the direction pad with its four choices providing only a jerky view of movements. How to get beyond this limit? The solution that they came up with involved a return to the principle of a miniature thumb-operated interface (the d-pad), and combining it with the continuity of knobs/paddles and the freedom of movement offered by the analog sticks from earlier generation of consoles. The patent thus describes the creation of a small lever that could be tilted with the thumb and which could be rotated through 360 degrees: the "thumb-stick". There are some concentric rings on the surface to prevent the thumb from slipping. Also, this lever has a mounting comprising an octagonal ring used as a guide mark (the possibility of moving in eight directions of space) to help the player, who no longer has to look at the lever to

79 - See also the Nintendo patent on the subject: U.S. patent #6017271: Three-dimensional image processing apparatus with enhanced automatic and user point of view of control.

80 - A "model and drawing" is a legal protection system covering the exterior appearance of a product or building. The model designated the product's three-dimensional exterior aspect, the drawing being the flat two-dimensional shape.

81 - U.S. patent #US376826: Controller for game machine.

82 - Giles Goddard, op. cit.

know where it is pointing. The advantage of this device thus lay in the crossing of two relevant earlier engineering principles: the joystick for its quality of control, and the direction pad for its easy manipulation that did not require the whole hand to grip a lever.

However, this analog stick was also an innovation in engineering terms, because, unlike the joysticks of the seventies, Nintendo opted this time not for a potentiometer but for complementary mechanical parts (lever, gears) and an optical system fitted with light emitting diodes to detect lever movements. So this was all closer to the way a mouse operates than to an Atari 5200 or Vectrex joystick, which used a potentiometer. The presence of these sensors got round the issue with breakages often encountered with joysticks on pre-1980 arcade game and home consoles by offering a more robust and hence longer-lasting system. For all that, mechanical glitches could still occur, either with the stick locking in one direction or the whole unit rotating erratically on account of worn internal components.

The creation of this analog stick also sparked an interesting controversy in the history of video games: was it the game design that influenced the invention of this solution? Or was it the new engineering principle that led to the creation of some novel gameplays? The game designers in the Myiamoto team claim the former is the correct version, recalling how: "We knew that we wanted characters to be able to move in the 3-D world in certain ways, and that determined what the controller had to be able to do. So yes, we were involved from a gaming point of view.[83] » But developers like Giles Goddard maintain the opposite: *"The actual movement of Mario came from the N64 controller, the way you move the central stick.[84]"*

Unfortunately, in light of the available documents, it is hard to tell which side to take. Having said that, the truth of the matter most likely lies somewhere in the middle, because designing as complex an engineering device as a video game console requires a long enough time for the various people concerned to exchange information, put forward constraining features and solutions, while

83 - "The game guys", Nintendo Power Vol. 80, 1996.

84 - Giles Goddard, op. cit.

taking on board the needs and wishes of everyone, be they hardware engineers, developers, game designers or marketing specialists. This hypothesis is borne out by the list of inventors named on the Nintendo 64 game controller patent. The fact that they are a game designer (Shigeru Myiamoto), a hardware engineer (Kenichiro Ashida), a programmer (Yasunari Nishida) and a hardware-software integration engineer (Genyo Takeda, head of the R&D3 department) clearly shows that the design of the analog stick, and more generally of the game controller, was a collective effort crystallizing all their individual contributions. To put it another way, the game controller and the game Super Mario 64 (1996) were designed simultaneously, with the development of the one affecting the other and vice-versa.

The Nintendo 64 joypad design and presentation was shrouded in great secrecy[85] at the various video games fairs in the mid-nineties. Although not so popular as the previous consoles[86], the Nintendo 64 was a landmark console owing to the return of the analog stick. Notably, because it was the start of a new line that is still going strong today.

Follow-my-leader with the analog stick

With the revival of the analog stick, we again find something already encountered during the eighties: a follow-my-leader attitude among Nintendo's competitor brands. SEGA was the first off, with a new version of the game controller on its Saturn (HSS-0137) console. Called the "Multi Controller" in Japan and the "3D pad" everywhere else, it was released in 1996 and sold as a package with the game Nights into Dreams.

The first joypad with this console released in 1994, so before the Nintendo 64, was an upgrade of the Mega Drive console, with six buttons. For the following version, as we saw in the previous chapter, SEGA opted for a rounded shape on which we find a direc-

---

85 - Some even tell the story of the game controller having been hidden in a cardboard box so that visitors could not see it!

86 - There are several reasons for this: no backward compatibility with earlier console games, a "cartridge" format that was poorer than the competition's CD-ROMs, a lack of interest among third party publishers, etc.

tion pad, six action buttons and... an analog stick in the shape of a rounded hemisphere.

Unlike the Nintendo, the game controller had a switch to select the stick or d-pad interface, which mean that players had to pick a navigation mode before they started. Another notable fact was that this SEGA controller did not use an optical system, but an ingenious magnet system that was more robust than on the competition's pads. Designed for Nights into Dreams with which it was sold, this stick made for smoother movements in the "flying" sections of the game than the d-pad did. This interaction quality, along with finer control and better adjusted trajectories, then made it possible to adapt it for car racing games (Daytona USA: Champion Circuit Edition, 1996; SEGA Touring Car Championship, 1996) and first-person shooting games (Quake, 1996; Doom, 1993). This model was a forerunner to the analog stick on the game controller of the next console, the Dreamcast, in November 1998.

In April 1997, it was Sony's turn to bring out a game controller with two analog sticks. Based on a system of potentiometers as on the Atari 5200 controllers, they could be selected with a switch, as on the SEGA Saturn. The patent filed by Teiyu Goto and Hiroki Ogata, the two Sony engineers in charge of this joypad, indicates that the purpose of this innovation was to facilitate the possibility for players of having their characters "rotatable in a 360° direction", "enabling analog movements such as combined rotation and linear movement, linear movement with a variable speed or change of the configuration of the display character", of "varying the line of sight of the display character", and lastly, of getting "a higher simulated reality feeling."[87]. This moreover was not by chance since the first games produced for use with this stick were fighting games (Tobal 2, 1997; and Bushido Blade, 1997). Previously, the only solution that the developers had come up with was to use the d-pad in a different way than was originally intended. This can be seen by watching a game like Resident Evil (1996): you press the up or down arrow to make the character move forward or backward. On the other hand, if the player presses the left or right directional arrow, the character does not move in that direction,

87 - U.S. patent #6231444: Operating device for game machine.

but the character's body pivots to the desired side.

In addition, it is not clear why Sony opted to use a double analog stick rather than just a single one. But the idea would seem to have been to offer an emulation of an old peripheral released a year before: the PlayStation Analog Joystick (SCPH-1110). Better known as the Sony Flightstick, this was a set of two joysticks that could each be operated with the whole hand and were designed for various arcade games (MechWarrior 2: 31st Century Combat, 1995; Top Gun: Fire at Will, 1996)[88]. This joystick was notably intended for flight simulators, and two sticks were needed in order to be realistic enough. Sony also used twin sticks on the Dual Analog pad although without giving them much to do in the first few games on offer. It was the advent of first-person shooting games that later encouraged people to use them together.

Notice how the simultaneous use of two analog sticks had already been explored in the arcade game Robotron: 2084 developed by William Electronics in 1982. In this shooting game, the player controlled a robot moving around a grid. Eugene Jarvis, the game's designer, found it frustrating to be performing both actions with just one joystick. So he had the bright idea of using one of the sticks to move the character and the other to fire with. The same publisher revived the experience with a remake of Robotron on the N64 (1998), for which the player had to use two joypads, one in each hand, so as to emulate the arcade version.

Still on this two-stick basis, Sony went on to design the next models with the "Dual shocks" series. Unlike the precursor, Dual Analog, the designers opted for a convex shape with an anti-skid gum material for the thumbs, which work overtime on such a device. Another notable change, the two sticks were more than just navigation interfaces, they were also buttons that the player could press, further extending the repertoire of available actions.

Be that as it may, another novelty with this double stick was its position on the game controller, with these two interfaces placed symmetrically right under the player's thumbs. This setup was

---

88 - These double joysticks were fashionable at the time since SEGA also had a similar arcade game (Cybertroops / Virtual ON, 1995) which was then transferred to the SEGA Saturn with the Twin Stick (HSS-0154, 1996) bearing a close resemblance to Sony's SCPH-1110.

crucial, because it created a second level of interaction easy to access while holding the controller. The player could use the thumbs to operate either the two sticks or the alternative "pad + buttons" configuration, or again a combination of both (operating the left stick and a button with the left thumb). This engineering feature thus enabled a new coding scheme[89] typical of 3D games: the left-hand stick generally controlling the character's movements, while the second controlled the camera and/or taking aim in shooting games. In a few exceptional instances (Katamari Damacy, 2004), the two sticks could also control the character's movements like the caterpillar tracks on a tank.

After 1997, the double analog stick option became an established standard, as we find it on joypads of the official consoles. The Nintendo designers soon came over to it, with the GameCube controller: the four yellow camera ("C") buttons on the N64 having been "merged" into a single analog stick of that color. The Nintendo Wii (Classic controller and Classic controller Pro) and Wii U (Classic controller Pro) pads revert to the symmetrical stick positions, and so does the Sony Dual Shocks line. With these models, we note how Nintendo was won over to the standard configuration of the majority intended for the more demanding regular player. As Katsuya Eguchi, senior producer and hardware producer of the Wii U reminds us: "adding a Pro controller may make it easier for multi-platform games to come out on the system. Wii remotes don't have things like analog sticks. To make it as easy as possible to enjoy certain multiplayer experiences it was important to have that Pro controller. We're all gamers as well and we appreciate the interest of those [hardcore] gamers, and we don't want them to feel left out, so we're making big strides and changes in that area.[90]"

With Microsoft on the other hand, the Xbox and Xbox 360 pads have an asymmetrical configuration, with the right-hand stick lower than the left-hand one (being symmetrical with the d-pad). This difference in the way the sticks are laid out is actually the

---

89 - When a game designer talks of a coding scheme, he is referring to the correspondence between the game controller buttons and the actions performed by the character on the screen.

90 - Interview with Gameplanet, 2012.

source of endless bickering between those who swear by Microsoft and all the others.

But notice how the symmetrical presence of the two analog sticks on the Dual Shock pads can have some unforeseen consequences. In fact, among the various ways of diverting video game controllers, there is one that involves wrapping elastic bands round the sticks to produce continuous movement in the game. This practice came in especially for games like Katamari Damacy, for which you have to rotate an increasingly large ball.

Alongside this standard form comprising two analog sticks, also worth mentioning are three engineering principles used by hardware manufacturers during the nineties to extend the range of navigation options in video games. Each in fact follows on from earlier technologies that are described in Chapter One of this book.

They include switches with the SNK Neo Geo CD Pad comprising an analog stick with eight micro-switches, enabling movements in that many directions. As is obvious now that this solution is no longer used, it was a temporary engineering principle inherited from arcade joysticks; for all its extra precision, this sort of stick was too fragile.

We should also mention the "circle pad", found on the Nintendo 3DS consoles that first appeared in February 2011, and on the Wii U prototype game controller presented at E3 in 2011. Based on the "drawing and model" filed at the US Patent Office[91], it represents a notable upgrade of the NES Max "cycloid" that came out in 1988. It comes in the shape of a small round protuberance that can be moved in every direction of the plane, like a thinner version of an analog stick. From a technical viewpoint, it is a combination of two potentiometers detecting movements in the two directions of the plane (vertical and horizontal). This feature in fact places it in the lineage of analog joysticks in the early days of video games; it is a stick with a rod so thin that it is flattened. Also we again find a similar-looking interface on games transferred to touch screens on smartphones and tablets. The circle pad then appears transparently, as a graphic element that is superimposed on the game world and it can be operated by the user, with no feeling of touching anything but a screen.

Lastly, and more unusually, the pad on the Pippin, an ill-fated project for a pad from Apple and Bandai in the mid-nineties, comprised a trackball offering an analog control mode. Having been designed both as a game apparatus and a home multimedia platform, the Pippin had an operating system derived from the current Mac OS 7 system, which required an analog interface similar to a mouse to use its graphic interface. Following on from the use of trackballs on the arcade games of the 1970s[92], this however was only a one-off on a console and there were few subsequent attempts to bring back such an engineering principle.

The one exception was a by-product of the Trackball featured in the SpaceTec brand's "SpaceOrb 360" released in 1996 and designed for 3D games. This game controller had a fairly standard shell with rounded edges on which a ball was mounted giving unbroken movement through six axes. Although Logitech produced two similar joypads, the Cyberman and the Cyberman II, after taking over SpaceTec, this type of peripheral remained a footnote. Meanwhile, the HKS Racing Controller from the Eagle3 company offers a kind of one-directional trackball for use in car racing games. It is a small push-pull type potentiometer that can be moved along a diagonal on the left-hand part of the pad and is used to simulate the turning of a car steering-wheel.

Motion sensors and pointing

While the return of the analog stick and its later persistence are a notable event in the history of video games, the combination of motion sensing and optical pointing technologies marked an even bigger breakthrough. Here again, the priority was not so much engineering logic as seeking to create novel gaming experiences.

As we saw in the previous chapter with our thoughts on the shape of the Wii interface, after the GameCube, what the Nintendo

---

92 - They are to be found to this day on Japanese Sangokushi Taisen type arcade machines.

designers wanted to do was to make the gaming experience more accessible. The Kyoto brand wanted to stand apart from the competition caught up in a frantic race to increase their machines' computing power, and so opted for a different approach aimed at winning over first-time users; or to be more precise, people who did not play video games. With the increasing complexification of game controllers since the Famicom, they realized that this was a major barrier for reaching the non-playing public. Hence the Nintendo executives saw the relevance of seeking to simplify their interfaces.

To achieve this aim for "intuitiveness", the strategy set in place by the team in charge of the project involved designing a peripheral that put combinations of buttons to one side and gave direct access immediately upon first trying out the console. Owing to the technical advances made in the early 2000s, the detection of users' gestures soon proved to be the best way of overcoming this problem[93]. As we humans are used to acting by making movements, why not use them on the screen? Why not offer a direct correspondence between our gestures in physical space and the ones appearing on the screen? These are the issues that the Wii designers were grappling with at the time.

Hence the next proposition was to capture movements made by players, mimicking motions and actions subsequently represented on the screen. But as the Nintendo boss states, the idea was not limited to video games, but more broadly to create "things that respond in fun ways to human input.[94]"

Hence the Wii interface comprised several engineering principles that are different from the ones we have described so far. So it definitely marks a break with the state of the art in the field of gaming peripherals. As the first piece in the puzzle, the Wiimote is made up primarily of a 3D accelerometer[95]. This is used to detect the player's movements by measuring acceleration in the three

---

93 - On this, see one of the Wii patents: US patent #20070066394: Video Game System with wireless modular handheld controller.

94 - Cited in Steven E. Jones and George K. Thiruvathukal, Codename revolution: The Nintendo Wii Platform, MIT Press, 2012.

95 - To be precise, a three-axis ADXL330 accelerometer manufactured by Analog Devices, as described in the press release Analog Devices and Nintendo Collaboration drives Videogame Innovation with IMEMS Motion Signal Processing Technology.

dimensions of space. This information is then sent to the console in realtime via a Bluetooth wireless connection. As an addition, a pointing device in the form of a sensor[96] on the end of the Wiimote locates up to two hundred times a second the infrared signal emitted by the light emitting diodes present in the sensor bar placed next to the screen. This enables the position at which the object is pointing to be calculated. This information is also sent to the console via Bluetooth to provide an accurate representation of the Wiimote's position facing the screen. The original device was then enhanced with the addition of the Wii Motion Plus[97] in 2009. This add-on mounted onto the bottom of the Wiimote made it possible to improve the precision of motion detection, notably with a better assessment of rotations of the wrist.

Historically speaking, the Nintendo designers had already turned to gestural interfaces with games intended for the Game Boy Advance: Yoshi's Universal Gravitation (2004), WarioWare: Twisted! (2004), Koro Koro Puzzle Happy Panechu! (2002), or for the Game Boy Color with Koro Koro Kirby (2000). The cartridges for these games included a piezoelectric gyroscopic sensor designed by NEC detecting when the portable console was tipped forward or raised toward the player. Such a system enabled swinging movements to be detected very simply. Moreover it was the hardware designer in charge of Kirby Tilt'n'Tumble, Akio Ikeda, who worked on building the accelerometers into the Wiimote. We may also recall how the video game is not the first area to latch onto these capture technologies: quite the opposite, we find applications dating back twenty years in areas as varied and the triggering of airbags in cars or computing the tilt on tilting trains.

Meanwhile, the Nunchuk, the Wii's secondary interface, comprises an analog stick similar to the GameCube stick, and an accelerometer[98] that measures both the peripheral's movements and its tilt. Connected to the Wiimote with a cable, the Nunchuk thus needs no pointing device as it uses the Wiimote's. Any information detected with this sensor is sent to the console via

---

96 - This is a CMOS (Complementary Metal-Oxide Semiconductor) sensor.

97 - Comprising an MEMS gyrometer, the IDG-600 made by the InvenSense company.

98 - An MEMS LIS3L02AL manufactured by the Franco-Italian company ST Microelectronics.

Bluetooth and compared with a database of possible movements in the game being played (throwing a bowl in a game of bowls, a tennis forehand etc.).

While the Wiimote and the Nunchuk do indeed mark a break in terms of the engineering principles conventionally applied in previous video games peripherals, we need however to qualify everything that has been said and written about the so-called revolution when the Wii was released in 2006. Indeed, if we observe the positioning of this innovation over the long term of research into digital interfaces and of earlier products in the field of video gaming, we realize that these two peripherals are both the fruit of a slowly maturing technology and its injection into the collective imagination through science-fiction movies like Minority Report (2002). Their novelty comes from the fact that these interfaces were the majority peripheral on the Wii console. Unlike earlier attempts, their success in terms of sales and utilization also shows how a new level had been reached in appropriating gestural interfaces.

However, we may recall how this type of gestural interface is part of a larger body of research into MMI that has been striving since the mid-eighties to get computing away from the monitor and standard peripherals (keyboard, mouse, optical pen...). In this area we see a broad range of achievements including virtual reality interfaces such as gloves simulating hands capturing an object, or "tangible interfaces"[99], which propose that elements of our environment become a way of controlling a computer program. With this in mind, think for instance of those projects for interactive tables or everyday items turned into computer interfaces. Such an approach was explored back in the eighties in the video games industry, with projects for a ground sheet as an ancestor to Dance Dance Revolution (1998) like the Foot Craz control pad (Exus) for the Atari VCS or the Family Trainer (same principle, but for the Famicom in 1986).

99 - Hiroshi Ishii and Brygg Ullmer, Tangible bits: towards seamless interfaces between people, bits and atoms, Proceedings of the SIGCHI97 conference on Human factors in computing systems, 1997.

Later on, this was also the case with the Power Glove distributed by Mattel[100] (1989). Fitted with ultrasound emitters, this glove was used to detect a player's gestures, through three sensors placed around the monitor. This product was one of the landmark flops of video games interfaces, notably on account of the lack of games using this peripheral, along with a lack of precision in sensing movements. In 1993, SEGA and Interactive Light had also experimented with motion sensors, with the SEGA Activator for the Mega Drive console. Based on the musician Assaf Gurner's experimental musical instrument the Light Harp, it was an octagonal mat composed of infrared diodes projecting this light onto the ceiling. The movements of the player placed in the center stopped the beam and were detected by the system. Here again, this product was unfortunately another commercial flop because of the lack of titles, its rather inflexible technology (requiring flat ceilings) and its greedy power consumption.

Moreover, the inclusion of motion sensors in a game controller is another research area that was explored during the nineties. At Nintendo, a project for a joypad of this type had been prototyped for the Nintendo 64, to no avail. In 1996, in filing the patent[101] for the Saturn 3D Pad, SEGA too had intended to add motion sensors into the game controller. It was not until 2000 that we saw the first accelerometer in a commercial product from a major video game manufacturer. This was the game Kirby Tilt 'n' Tumble (2000) on the Game Boy Color, which included a sensor actually inside the cartridge, in order to be able to play while tilting the portable console in the chosen direction to move the character.

The genealogy of the Wiimote also has to take into account earlier products using optical detection and the expertise that Nintendo had built up in these technologies since the early seventies. The first optical guns that the Kyoto firm brought out in 1973, and the Beam Gun on the Famicom released in 1984 (NES Zapper on the NES in 1985), as well as the Nintendo R.O.B robot (Robot Operating Buddy) in 1985, should all be seen as optical interfaces.

---

100 - And designed by Grant Goddard and Samuel Cooper Davis of the Abrams Gentile Entertainment company (AGE).

101 - U.S. patent #7488254: Controller and expansion unit for controller.

They prepared the ground for more complex forms such as the Wiimote pointing device[102]. Each of these appliances in fact operated with a system sensing the light emitted by a remote source (television or other screen). When the player pressed the trigger, the console detected where on the screen the pistol was being aimed, and hence the targets hit could be modified, for example by blowing them up. On the Wiimote, the CMOS sensors on the end operate on similar lines.

Likewise, the use of 2D cameras such as Sony's EyeToy on the PS2 (2003) or Logitech's webcams offered an alternative to Nintendo's choices for gesture detection. It was actually by exploring this avenue further that Microsoft[103] devised their Kinect project (2010). Based on the combination of a 3D camera developed by the Israeli company PrimeSense with an infrared optical detection system, this interface also provided fine sensing of players' movements or facial and object recognition. As it is not strictly speaking a joypad, we shall not be going into the details on this point... except to say that the special feature of these devices is that they do away with the game controller and invite you to use the whole body as a gaming interface.

To come back to proper joypads, only Sony have ventured into designing game controllers comprising sensors and cameras. Through their presence in electronics for the general public and in robotics, these research and development engineers have in fact developed several motion detection technologies that were later integrated within their interfaces. To start with, the official PS3 pad, the Sixaxis model (2006), was like a trial run. In terms of its shape, it was a more elaborate Dual Shock 2, one that included a motion sensor detecting six possible directions of movement through space (forward/reverse, up/down, left/right)[104]. Despite its sensitive motion detection capability, this was an option that game developers ultimately had little time for.

---

102 - For a more detailed discussion on this subject, see Steven E. Jones and George K. Thiruvathukal, op. cit.

103 - Although Microsoft places the emphasis on the 3D camera, the company's engineers have also filed a number of patents for interfaces with accelerometers.

104 - A MEMS 3-axis accelerometer (Hokuriku HAAM0325B) and a MEMS vibrating piezo-electric gyrometer (Murata ENC-03R).

The next model, called PlayStation Move (2010), was based on a more radical innovation. Like Nintendo, its designers, led by engineer Richard Marks, gambled on having a simpler interface to attract non-players who might otherwise be put off by the joypad. Offering a peripheral made up of two parts, one held in each hand, the adopted principle is fairly similar to the Wiimote/Nunchuk combination. Technically speaking, these two elements are operated with an EyeToy camera capable of detecting light emitted by the colored globe on the end of the "PlayStation Move motion controller". In this way, the system determines the game controller's absolute position in the three dimensions of space, including depth. Having the camera is also interesting, as it can also detect the entire body and

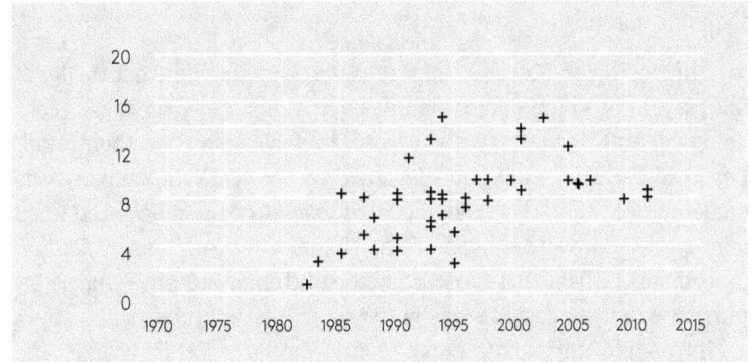

Figure 31: Increase of the surface area dedicated to navigation.

not just the presence of the controllers in its field of vision. This is an interesting approach because it enables the machine's response to be fine-tuned for certain games. This "motion controller" also comprises a combination of sensors[105] that can make a rather accurate assessment of the player's gestures. As Sony wanted to make the second peripheral, called the "navigation controller", optional, it had no special sensors and made do with a direction pad, an analog stick, two buttons and two triggers.

---

105 - A 3-axis gyrometer (measuring rotations), a 3-axis accelerometer (evaluating accelerations) and a magnetometer (measuring the direction and intensity of a magnetic field).

Carrying on from the Wii or Move, the Wii U console released by Nintendo in the fall of 2012 presents a new peripheral: the Game-Pad. Apart from the touch screen, about which more later, it comprises two symmetrical analog sticks, a direction pad and various action and selection buttons, triggers and a combination of sensors[106] and a camera. From the standpoint of motion detection, the appliance carries on from the Wiimote. Combined with the sensors, the screen on the controller is innovative in terms of navigating in gaming spaces. On the few titles available when the console first came out, this screen provides other different viewpoints on the game world, for instance by showing what is going on around the scene being watched on the TV set (360° vision). It can also display what is happening behind the backs of the players represented on the main screen.

In closing on gestural interfaces, let us remember that the leading players in video games do not have a monopoly on these technologies, and third party manufacturers have also tried their hand. For example, the "Bodypad" designed by the XK Pad company was made up of straps to be added on at the level of the elbow and knee joints; on them were sensors in the shape of buttons that picked up movements. Given that these detector-buttons were pretty basic affairs, the motion capture was not very sensitive, obliging players to go into some unrealistic contortions. Similarly, other brands like Razer (with its Hydra for PC) or Nyko (with its Wand for the Nintendo Wii) have offered various peripherals that have generally met with little success. On this subject, SEGA even sold under its own brand a "SEGA Reactor" consisting of a SEGA Mega Drive including about twenty games and controllable with a game controller having a motion sensor!

Finally, the last type of player in the world of gestural interfaces, the makers of southern Asian counterfeits have been especially active in the production of cheap copies of the Wii. Think for example of the Vii (Chintendo), The Zone or the Miwi 9800 (Eittek Electonics). The games sold for these consoles, all based on special hardware that is different from its colleague's, are obviously very

---

106 - A 3-axis gyrometer, a 3-axis accelerometer, an NFC radiofrequency sensor and a Bluetooth connection.

low quality. But for an outside observer, the poor quality of these products is evidence of the relative difficulty in striking a balance between the technological dimension (sensors that are basically cheap) and the creation of games that are esthetically pleasing or fun to play.

An evolution in three stages

The evolution of means of navigation in joypads brings out three main stages comprising in succession: the direction pad, the analog stick, then gesture detection. Looking at current game controllers moreover, we see how these different choices did not replace each other[107] since all three feature on certain joypads (Sony Sixaxis). We are talking more about an accumulation of these interfaces either on the pad (d-pad, stick) or inside it (sensors). So much so that we see the surface area allocated to character movements on the game controller physically growing, as shown in Figure 31. The combination of these three control modes is not just ornamental, it results from a need to maintain a degree of versatility in the peripheral by allowing three means of control. Owing to the diversity of existing games, it was important to preserve these different types, as some games are simply unplayable with any one of them. Navigating in a 3D world for instance is not easy with a direction pad.

From an evolutionary standpoint, we may note the continuous nature of the evolution of these navigation interfaces. Each of them is the outcome of applying earlier engineering principles. Switches, potentiometers, optical sensors and accelerometers have featured on numerous occasions in the past history of video games or arcade games, in the form of either products or a prototype. So their insertion in the game controller was a gradual affair, with increasing complexification.

These various elements evidence conventional aspects of the way engineering objects evolve. First we note the presence of hybridizations with the direction pad, resulting from a set of switches

---

107 - With the exception of Microsoft Kinect.

combining together; or the analog stick that can notably comprise several potentiometers. You also see revivals with the return of the joystick in miniature form, or the presence of optical sensors on recent interfaces like the Wiimote or Sony Move. So these may have been influenced by innovations made by competitors.

In addition, the "circulation" of certain options is also evidence of the variable "clout" of the different makers in terms of innovation and stabilizing these interfaces. In this regard, the elements described in this chapter bring out the pioneering nature of the Nintendo interfaces throughout their history. The Kyoto brand thus seems to be ahead of the competition at every stage. Having said that, we should not however understated the importance of the achievements of SEGA in its day, and more recently of Sony or Microsoft. Because each of these corporations has also contrived to adapt and enhance some of the principles tried and tested by Nintendo. Seeing the double analog stick arranged symmetrically on the Dual Shock 2 and 3 game controllers, and the way the Nintendo designers subsequently turned to this option with the Wii U, we realize how ingenious this was.

Above and beyond technical considerations relating to these three major stages, it should be stressed that with all these navigating means there is a corresponding view of the players and what they might be able to do. From the standpoint of game design, each of the joypads refers back to what we call a "spatial script". We take this term[108] to mean the way in which game designers imagine that players move around the world depicted on the screen. Looking at a Famicom pad, we realize how simple that spatial script is, as there is just a d-pad with which to make discrete moves in four directions. At the other extreme, a Sixaxis game controller with two analog sticks, a direction pad and an accelerometer allows for much more varied and complex control of one's movements.

For each joypad, and for each video game that uses it, we could likewise decode the ways in which the game and hardware designers have imagined movements through space. If such an analysis were to be carried out it would likely show how the spatial script has evolved in the direction of making things more lifelike. Indeed,

108 - Inspired by the sociology of engineering techniques, particularly the "script" notion as described by Madeleine Akrich.

broadly speaking, the three stages that we have described in this chapter tend to point toward increasing fine-tuning of on-screen navigation. With the direction pad, motion is only possible along two axes, and it is intermittent. With the analog stick, movements become continuous and through several dimensions of space. Lastly, with gestural interfaces, physical movements become the input peripheral. And, while there is still a stage of processing the gesture performed by the player, the outcome can appear more subtle than with a stick[109].

It is important to note this gradual modification to the spatial scripts, because this is how we become aware that designing a joypad and its navigation interfaces is more than just accumulating various different technologies; other factors have had an influence as well. To sum up this chapter, the d-pad design was brought about by a desire on the part of the line management to distance themselves from earlier products and to enrich gameplay with movements and simultaneous actions (marketing and game design factor). Meanwhile, the insertion of motion sensors in the Wiimote came about through a desire for a clean break with the earlier interfaces (marketing or strategic factor). Nonetheless, technical possibilities and constraints can also influence the spatial script, as was the case with the use of accelerometers in the Wiimote or the Sony Move. Lastly, the legacy of previous interfaces, and the habits that they have instilled in players can also affect the definition of this spatial script. In this category, we may think notably of the revival of analog sticks.

109 - On the subject of the comparison between gestural interfaces and the pad, we find differences in the experiences that players have depending on their level of skill. See notably Nicolas Nova and Timothée Jobert, Intuitivité et incorporation des interactions gestuelles chez les utilisateurs de jeux vidéo, Proceedings of the IHM09 Conference, 2009.

Part 4 - Action

Alongside navigation interfaces, the actions that players can perform, made possible by the presence of buttons, have also had an influence. With a cursory look at the evolution of game controllers, we soon realize that their history points to an increase in the number of action buttons. From the Famicom to the latest pad models, we indeed see a rapid accumulation that has since settled down to a fixed number of buttons over the last few years. We may also observe the search for ingenious solutions for arranging them without making the object an unusable mess.

Just as it is possible to read the representation of space in the game controller, an analysis of the action buttons enables the way the gaming possibilities have evolved to be deciphered. This chapter describes this gradual complexification and pauses to ponder the meaning that game designers give to each of these interfacing elements.

The two original buttons

Since we have taken the Famicom as the first joypad, this is the one we shall be looking at in order to understand the basic configuration of the action buttons.

As we saw in the chapter on the shape of game controllers, the Famicom joypad design was influenced by the interfaces of the Game & Watch electronic games designed by the R&D1 unit at Nintendo. In particular it was the two-screen Donkey Kong (1981) model, with its d-pad and action button located on the right that are behind it. One of the innovations on the Famicom game controller was the addition of two system control buttons ("select" and "start") and an extra action button. This button seems to have emerged from discussions among the game design team, who wanted to offer a broader variety of gameplays than with the Game & Watch games, and which thus required a somewhat more elaborate interface.

To each of these two buttons distinct actions could be allocated. In Super Mario Bros, they were used for jumping (button A), running (button B held down) or throwing fireballs (button B pushed briefly). In other games, pressing both A and B made further actions possible as well (or the use of "cheat codes", generally a word or combination of keys to be entered to win a bonus or some special power). So this was the birth of the "combos", or button combinations to create actions to optimize the utilization of these interfaces without having to add on a dedicated button each time.

Moreover, on the first version of the Famicom game controller, the two action buttons were originally square. Unfortunately, and despite Nintendo's pernickety test procedures, their shape meant that they sometimes became stuck in the down position. As Masayuki Uemura, director of Nintendo's second research and development unit (R&D2) in charge of designing the console, states: "Another problem were the square buttons on the controller. They would get stuck down. [...] We hadn't expected them to see so much. [...] I don't think we really understood how people play home video games. We solved the button problem by making the square buttons round, but I think players were using more force with their fingers than when using Game & Watch.[110] » The solution they found to this problem involved using rounded buttons, a shape that later became standard, with the exception of a few models (GameCube, Jaguar, XBox).

Another notable feature of the Famicom game controller, then the NES, which adopted the same configuration, concerns the way of naming these two buttons. Most of the game controllers of the time in fact had no special labeling. Only the Vectrex or the Intellivision displayed figures on or next to the buttons. With a view to greater clarity for users and to be different from Atari, Nintendo chose to give them names[111]. On the other hand, their choice is somewhat surprising, since Uemura's team called the button on the far right, near the edge, button "A", and "B" the one to its left. Hence the familiar "BA" setup that was again found on subsequent pads and on the Game Boy models. There are a variety of

110 - Interview "Iwata asks", op. cit.

111 - David Sheff, **Game Over: Press Start to Continue**, Cyberactive Media Group, 1999.

interpretations to account for this choice. The most-often cited is that "A" being the dominant action button, it was more logical and comfortable to place it on the right, just under the position where the thumb would be.

On controllers of consoles of the same generation (SEGA Mark III/Master System, Atari 7800, NEC PC Engine), the makers also opted for two buttons in addition to the direction pad. While the Atari designers left them nameless, at SEGA they soberly called them 1 (start) and 2. Meanwhile NEC chose Roman numerals "I" and "II", ultimately not very different from the reversed alphabetical positioning "B" and "A" on the Famicom. The pad's overall shape, the presence of a d-pad (albeit modified) and these two buttons thus indicate how the competition tended to toe Nintendo's line.

War of the Buttons

With the arrival of the next generation, on consoles using the 16-bit processor, a button race then started, lasting until the late nineties.

While Nintendo maintained its position as market leader during the eighties with just a single console, the Famicom (and its NES model outside of Japan), the engineers at SEGA were busy bringing out no less than five different models of console[112]. Under Hideki Sato, the head of the R&D department, their task of catching up with their Kyoto rival was no easy matter, and the only way to succeed was to pull off a major coup that offered something completely different. This is why the design of the Mega Drive console[113] (1988) moved away from imitating Nintendo's projects, the way SEGA's Mark III or Master System had done with their very similar interfaces to the Famicom. Apart from the console's technical power, being an upgrade of the System-16 arcade machine, the break was mainly to do with the item's design, notably including the joypad. While the overall look is different, the designers also broke new ground with the number of buttons.

112 - Respectively: SG-1000, SG-1000 II, Mark III, SC-3000/H, and the Master System.

113 - Owing to the existence of another technology company called Mega Drive Systems, Inc., this console was given a different name in the USA (SEGA Genesis).

For the Mega Drive game controller (1988) had three buttons, initially called triggers, and named A, B and C respectively. They were placed along a sloping line on the surface of the pad, under a Start button. This console and its interface reflected the SEGA designers' intention not just to upgrade the home console, but also to capitalize on their experience with arcade games. This of course involved porting games, as well as producing suitable hardware for them. But that these required more than two buttons was really nothing new. So the proposed break by SEGA was to add on elements to the interface: first of all a third action button, with the initial model that came with the newly released console, then six with the porting of the arcade game Street Fighter II Dash (1993). Thus the influence of arcade games was behind the innovative path taken by the designers at SEGA. With a market share in 16-bit consoles reaching 55% in the US in the early nineties, unlike the Master System and its ancestors, the Mega Drive went on to stand as a serious rival to Nintendo. The quality of the games, the porting of arcade games and the new interface devoted to them very likely had a part in this success.

Alongside this, and after several years with no new console, Nintendo also set themselves the target of making a clean break with their new model, the Super Famicom (1991). In addition to the competition from SEGA with the Mega Drive, the collaboration between the entertainment publisher Hudson Soft and the maker NEC was another source of concern for the Nintendo executives and stirred them into innovating.

Here again, designing a new joypad for the Super Famicom to match the machine's more powerful technical capacity was also on the agenda. On a rounded shape which came up for discussion in Chapter 2, the designers set four action buttons in a diamond formation on the right. This group was arranged symmetrically in relation to the d-pad, and offered equivalent control, with the right thumb sitting naturally over it, allowing effective manipulation given the pad's user-friendly shape. Apart from one extra button compared with the Mega Drive, the designers of this game controller, guided by Masayuki Uemara, proposed one further modification: the addition of two buttons on the side (L and R), accessible with the left and right index fingers, was thus a novel feature[114]. These "shoulder buttons", as they were called, were an interesting feature of the interface, being based on the optimization of the controller surface, thereby ascribing a function to the edge of the pad, which had never been used before and thus becomes at once a way of resting the fingers on the pad and pressing action buttons as well. And the buttons are arranged naturally with respect to the pad's shape and how it is held.

According to Shigeru Miyamoto, head of game design with Nintendo, the number of buttons on the Super Famicom joypad came from the Capcom game Street Fighter II (1993)[115].

This emblematic arcade game of the time had a huge influence on the hardware since both Nintendo and SEGA designed their respective game controllers in order for it to be ported. As the Nintendo designers found adding six buttons onto the top of the pad overly complex, it was decided to split them into two groups, on the front and on the shoulder. As described in the patent for the Super Famicom game controller, the aim of Uemura's team was to allow slight movements of the hands holding the peripheral: *"various and many switches of the controller for a game machine of the present invention can be operated, with very little movement of hands of a player holding the controller[116]."* The idea was notably to minimize finger movement while keeping only slight freedom of movement for the index and middle fingers compared to the thumbs' much greater freedom.

This total of six action buttons on the game controller is equivalent to that of the second SEGA Mega Drive joypad released in 1993, only with a different layout. While the designers of this pad followed a logic similar to arcade games (buttons on the front), at Nintendo they adopted a different strategy with these shoulder buttons. This is in fact more of an upgrade of the Famicom pad through improved ergonomics than the hybridization of the joypad with the arcade gaming interface (SEGA's "façade logic").

---

114 - The patent for the Super Famicom game controller mentions that the middle finger can also be used for this purpose; U.S. patent #5207426: Controller for a game machine.

115 - Which is highly debatable given the priority of the Super Famicom console (released in 1990) over the arcade release of Street Fighter II (1991)!

116 - U.S. patent #5207426: Controller for a game machine.

So this evolution in the number of buttons evidences two distinct design approaches: the Nintendo designers, doing their own thing, taking the interface along a path of their own, and the SEGA designers, integrating the principle of a previous interface. The rival brands that NEC, Atari and Commodore were at the time then followed the lead as regards these two approaches. To quote just a few examples, note how the joypad on the PC-FX (NEC, 1994), in parallel with SEGA, replicated the layout of the six buttons on the Avenue Pad 6 game controller released on the PC Engine duo for playing Street Fighter II Dash. Following Nintendo's logic, the Amiga CD-32 (1993) pad had two buttons on the edge and four on the right side, arranged in squares, like the Super Famicom. As for the CD-i joypad, the designers at Philips reverted to the principle of four buttons in a diamond shape, but with no button on the shoulder. So this was a remake of the Super Famicom model without taking it to its logical conclusion. Only the game controller on the Panasonic 3DO (1993) can be considered to be a hybrid of the two approaches, with two shoulder buttons and three buttons on the front arranged as on the first Mega Drive joypad.

Later on, the buttons placed on the underside of the pad soon earned the nickname "triggers", being rather like gun triggers, and went on to become a standard feature on the Nintendo 64, Sony Dual Analog and Dual Shock 2, Microsoft XBox, etc. But most notable of all is the presence of this variation on the shoulder button on the Saturn (1994) as it demonstrates SEGA's conversion to this interface. Successive upgrades to these triggers is further evidence of Nintendo's ability time and time again to impose a standard interface, after the d-pad, and before the analog stick, while leaving the competition enough leeway to transform this shared benchmark.

As shown in Figure 32, also noteworthy is the way the mid-nineties marked the high point of the massive presence of buttons on game controllers. While the SEGA Saturn joypad with its eight buttons is a good example, Atari run out easy winners with no less than fifteen buttons on the Jaguar (and eighteen on the second version of that pad). Some of the buttons were located on the top right hand section of the pad, and worked with the thumb, while the twelve middle ones were centrally placed, unmarked and harder to get at.

1. Action buttons

a. circle

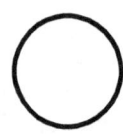

b. bean shape

c. thin curve

2. Menu buttons

a. rectangular

b. arrow

c. grain of rice

d. switch

e. rhombic

f. pill shape

3. Triggers

a. one, centred

d. two, centred, horizontal

b. one, off centred

c. two, centred, vertical

3. Triggers

e. two, centred, square format

f. four, centred

g. three, asymetric

h. four, symetric, different shapes

i. four, symetric, two horizontal and two vertical

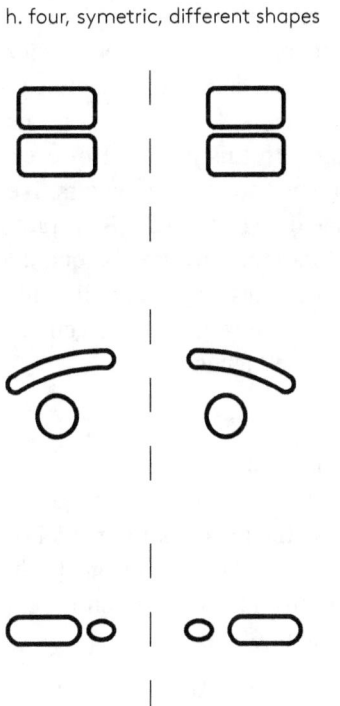

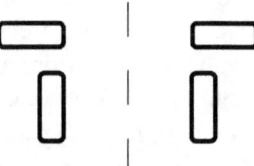

This momentary inflation corresponds to the major influence of arcade machines and console games during that decade. With advances in electronics and microengineering, and the arrival of more powerful processors and graphics boards, game designers at last had achieved porting of arcade games onto consoles. And accordingly, in so doing, hardware designers added extra complexity to home console interfaces, so much so that some became unplayable and were severely criticized by players; the Jaguar was the symbol of everything that was wrong with this period. However, such an approach was not always doomed to fail, as makers like SNK with the Neo Geo were meantime doing very well. By targeting a market of loyal arcade gamesters ready to pay for quality hardware, pricey game cartridges and expensive peripherals, this brand fared a lot better that Atari who were targeting the general public with an ill-adapted interface on the Jaguar.

After this decade of excesses, the number of action buttons and triggers gradually settled down in the late nineties. Things really calmed down quite considerably as the presentation model of the four buttons in a diamond shape on the Super Famicom slowly became the norm, as shown by successive PlayStation controllers and the siting of the buttons on the XBox 360.

Sony's case is relevant to this discussion in that it is based on an original design strategy. While taking over Nintendo's options (four front buttons in a diamond shape, with shoulder buttons), the designers at Sony led by Teyiu Goto adapted that interface, with the four buttons receiving their own iconography, being set in a kind of replica of the direction pad now engraved in the plastic housing, giving the game controller an overall symmetrical appearance. In addition, the shoulder buttons were doubled up (L1, R1, L2, R2), which made the game designers happy and the arcade game enthusiasts as well, as they were always needing more buttons. Here again, the presence of these shoulder buttons was ergonomically sound, providing easy access to the index and middle fingers.

Although we have no documents to explain such a follow-my-leader attitude, it may be due to the collaboration between the two Japanese makers over the aborted production of a CD-Rom player intended for the Super Famicom. Intended to compete with the SEGA MegaCD released in 1991, this first prototype called "Play Station" had been produced jointly and used the Super Famicom joypad.

After the project was ditched by Sony and Nintendo, Teyiu Goto's team put the benefit of this research to good use in making their own console, the PlayStation. Thus the number of buttons and their positioning on the controllers may have been influenced by the earlier collaboration, while coming in for a few adaptations.

Oddly enough, while this stabilized model seems to have become established starting with the Super Famicom for the Dual Shocks and Xbox pads, Nintendo's R&D teams nonetheless continued to innovate with several models deviating from the standard that they themselves had created. The configuration of the N64 pad and of the iQue, its equivalent on the Chinese market, is interesting in this connection. The buttons located on the top right section

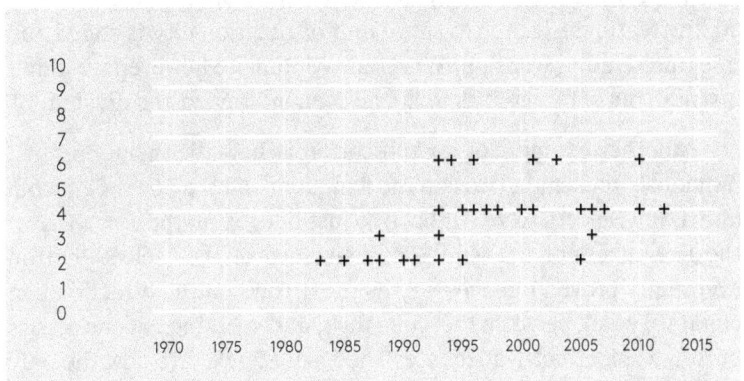

Figure 32: Evolution in the number of action buttons on joypads.

resemble the two rows of three buttons on the second joypad of the Mega Drive and the Saturn. They had six buttons including four yellow ones used to control the cameras. The patent for the N64 game controller[117] shows a configuration basically rather similar to that on the Saturn, with the six buttons aligned.

---

117 - U.S. patent USD376826: Controller for a game machine.

Nintendo's designers then reverted to their original arrangement since the GameCube had four action buttons on the front, in addition to the three triggers. But instead of the diamond-shaped layout, these were presented differently, with three small buttons surrounding a fourth, larger one. Apparently, in their effort toward ongoing enhancement, the designers at the Kyoto firm were never satisfied with their offering and were constantly tinkering with this type of detail. In the mid-2000s, with the Wii Classic pad and subsequent Wii joypads, we do note however some stabilization focusing on the four-button diamond, which had become just as powerful a standard as the direction pad and the double analog stick.

Lastly, even though the trend has been toward a stabilization of the number of buttons, the case of the Wiimote is interesting because it shows a one-off downsizing in order to come up with a less user-unfriendly interface. As Kenichiro Ashida, in charge of designing the game controller, recalls, "After all, our previous controllers, for the NES, SNES, N64 and GameCube, have evolved by adding features. That is to say, a unit of functionality is added and integrated into the design. With the Wii Remote however, we didn't just add, but subtracted as well, and even multiplied and divided.[118]"

Another example of simplification is how the menu buttons, previously present in twos on the Famicom and the Super Famicom (Start and Select), were cut back to just one, as on the Mega Drive, the Dreamcast or the N64. The existence of the "select" button eventually proved unnecessary as the arrows on the direction pad could very well perform the same task, and so a single menu access button was perfectly adequate. The Dual Shocks are now the only exception in this regard.

Towards button specialization

The above-described button evolution also highlights the underlying search for specialization. Ever since the Famicom joypad, the interface has presented a distinction between buttons A and B and the menus ("select", "start"). The introduction and

118 - Interview conducted by Video Games Blogger in May 2007.

Figure 33: Configuration of the N64 buttons according to the patent.

later generalization of shoulder buttons is another example. So, for game controller designers there are a variety of possible ways of differentiating buttons and their functions.

One initial specialization strategy involved where the buttons in question were placed and how they looked. Overall shape, surface, materials and colors are the list of features that designers combined into various possibilities. In this connection, the triggers placed on the edge of the controller offer the most obvious form of specialization. This frees up room on the front of the joypad, thereby avoiding over-using the thumbs, with the index and middle fingers helping out. Also, just like the d-pad and the buttons on the front right of the pad, they are placed where these fingers can be held over them in a natural hand position. This configuration is also interesting because for a beginner, the triggers are not as visible as the buttons on the front of the pad. For instance, buttons L3 or R3 on a Dual Shock 2 or 3 are seldom used, but having them is ultimately no problem, being out of players' sight. In other words, unskilled users just ignore them, while practiced players naturally place their fingers over them and know how to operate them, making these joypad models actually fairly versatile and suitable for various types of user.

Similarly, a quick glance at a Famicom or a PlayStation joypad is enough to spot the difference between the action buttons on the side and the menu buttons placed in the middle of the pad.

Being used less frequently, and not at all to manipulate the character on the screen, their positioning was of course a secondary consideration, hence in the middle of the pad, leaving the section of the game controller under the thumb of the right hand for the more commonly used action buttons. For further effect and to enable players to feel the difference without having to look, the shapes given to these buttons are different, as are the materials they are made of. From the soft rectangle with rounded corners on the Famicom to the central spherical Xbox logo on the Microsoft console, several approaches have been adopted.

Another example of differentiated action buttons relates to the choice of surface to give them: concave or convex. Thus the joypad on the Super NES, the North American version of the Super Famicom, was designed with two concave buttons (X and Y) and two convex buttons (A and B) so as to enable players to tell the difference by hand between the two extra buttons compared with the NES (X and Y). Nonetheless, except for the NES Max buttons and the GameCube triggers, since then few game controller designers have used this distinctive feature, as most buttons have been either flat or convex.

The use of colors is another method often encountered to distinguish between the different buttons. Hence, with the Super Famicom (Japan) and the Super Nintendo (Europe), the Nintendo designers came up with four distinct colors (and not two on the Super NES in North America) to help identify each button. Thus the colors for A, B, X and Y were respectively red, yellow, blue and green. This arrangement was actually used as a logo for that console. Commodore, SEGA, Neo Geo and Apple-Bandai then latched onto these same standard colors, although not necessarily in that order or with those names.

The most clearcut example of buttons with specialized shapes is definitely still the GameCube. The game controller for that console is a one-off in the history of joypads as the action buttons located on the right did not all look the same[119]. Gathered around an outsized central, round green A button, the round red button B

---

119 - A strategy that was also adopted, albeit less successfully, by Commodore with the Amiga CD32 game controller.

was placed underneath, and X/Y, in gray, were placed above in a bean shape. In an interview with the Nintendo design team, Satoru Iwata, the company chairman from 2000 explained the main reason for this layout: "He [Shigeru Miyamoto] was actually already thinking of ways to make the controller more accessible during the development of the GameCube. That's why there's a single large button that stands out on the GameCube controller, so the player knows which button to press first.[120]" The Nintendo game controller designers, along with Miyamoto (software) and Ashida (hardware) had in fact noticed how in most games, there was one button that you had to be pressing nearly all the time. So to highlight that button by giving it a special place, shape and color was a way of helping this function along. The rationale behind this was to have a specially dedicated interface for such basic actions as jumping or firing a gun.

The positioning of B, X and Y around this central button was also intended to minimize movements of the thumb away from the central A. So each of these three buttons could be dedicated to less frequent actions than the ones controlled by A; pressing B was used for secondary, less important actions and X/Y for still less crucial actions (dropping bombs in Mario 64 or to access a menu). In this way, the distance in relation to the thumb's natural position on the right-hand side of the pad reflected the level of importance of actions performed in the game. And this was in decreasing order of importance: A, B, Y then X.

With this organizational mode, it now became possible to create simple games for occasional players by asking them to interact with the central buttons only (analog stick, A, triggers) and just ignore buttons that were less accessible with the thumb (X, Y and possibly B). The game controller was thus somewhat versatile by allowing seasoned players to use the other buttons in the games dedicated to them. Moreover this target had another advantage since, being positioned above A, the X and Y keys made A/X and A/Y combinations very straightforward by pressing the thumb down more firmly to press both together.

120 - Interview in the "Iwata Asks" series.

For all its attractiveness, this organizational mode remains a footnote in the history of video gaming interfaces and no other game controller subsequently adopted it. One of the reasons generally put forward is to say that players were unhappy with the tricky manipulation of this non-standard button configuration for playing fighting games.

From an ergonomic standpoint, the GameCube controller remains an interesting witness to a principle regularly applied by interface designers: Fitts' Law[121]. Defined by the psychologist Paul Fitts in 1954, this model of human movement predicts that the time needed to go from a starting position to a final destination area depends on two factors: the distance to the target, and the size of the target. Transposing this to the case of the GameCube, this law states that the movement of the thumb from A to B is faster than from A to C, which is further away (intuitively correct) and, most of all, that the movement from B to A is faster than from B to C, which is the same distance away. So, while the recommendations drawn from Fitts' Law, such as enlarging a main target, are conventionally used in designing graphical interfaces (OS, Web pages), this is not so much in evidence with gaming peripherals since the GameCube is one of the few instances of its application.

Button nomenclature

Naming the buttons is a second way of reflecting their specialization. Over time, the different makers went down different paths, and this is worth reconstructing here.

With the advent of the very first joypads, the Nintendo designers opted to use letters (B and A) on the Famicom, while at SEGA and Atari they went for digits (1/start and 2) on the Master System and on the 7800 pad. With the PC Engine, the teams at NEC followed SEGA's logic by using a numbering system, only with Roman numerals (I and II). For the next generation, the SEGA designers joined those in favor of letters as the joypad for the Mega Drive had three alphabetical buttons A B C. On the other hand, when adding

121 - Paul M. Fitts, "The information capacity of the human motor system in controlling the amplitude of movement", Journal of Experimental Psychology, Vol. 47(6), 1954.

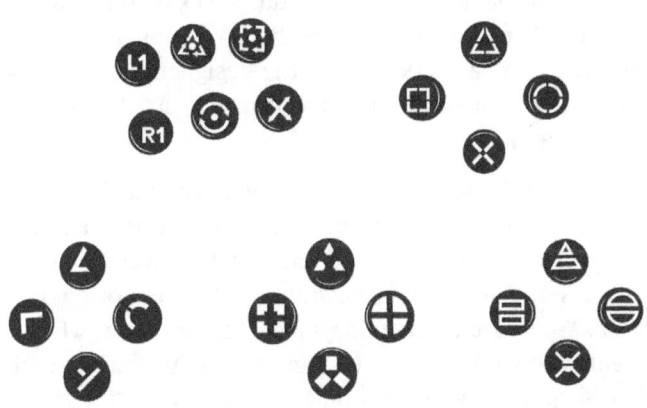

Figure 34: Panorama of copies of PlayStation symbols.

two action buttons onto the Super Famicom, the Nintendo designers used the letters ABXY. Why did they not do what SEGA did, which would have meant using C and D? One reason often mentioned was Nintendo's designers desire to have a naming system that could be expanded satisfactorily in a way that ABXY allowed, and ABCD did not, e.g. whenever extra buttons might be needed. However, the little documentary evidence we have is not always consistent, and this explanation remains no more than conjecture.

However mysterious the origin of ABXY, this was the option later upheld by Nintendo (on the GameCube, with a phase without X or Y on the N64) and which we again find with SEGA and then Microsoft. In the case of the triggers, the nomenclature was more straightforward, a question of lateralization guiding the choice of names: L and R, for Left and Right on the Super Famicom supplied the basis, and the addition of extra triggers quite simply led to a number being added on referring to it (L1/R1, L2/R2) on the Dual Shocks pads. Only the N64, GameCube and Wii pads used a Z trigger, a letter that does not follow the trigger nomenclature, but the ABXY one. Here again, the lack of documentation on this subject means that we have no explanation for this choice. That same Z later became ZL and ZR on the Wii Classic, L and R again indicating the trigger on the left or right.

While the names of the Nintendo, SEGA or Microsoft console game controllers are ultimately fairly conventional with the use of letters, the approach adopted by the designers of the Sony Dual Shocks, using symbols, is an interesting one, marking a break with the competition.

As Teiyu Goto, head of the Sony Corporate Design Center, recalls, this was a difficult decision, linked to the design team's to break new ground in a way relevant to players: "Other game companies at the time assigned alphabet letters or colors to the buttons. We wanted something simple to remember, which is why we went with icons or symbols, and I came up with the triangle-circle-X-square combination immediately afterward. I gave each symbol a meaning and a color. The triangle refers to viewpoint; I had it represent one's head or direction and made it green. Square refers to a piece of paper; I had it represent menus or documents and made it pink. The circle and X represent 'yes' or 'no' decision-making and I made them red and blue respectively. People thought those colors were mixed up, and I had to reinforce to management that that's what I wanted.[122]" In addition, for Japanese players, the cross (batsu) and the circle (maru) are not just geometric shapes, these symbols have a readily decoded meaning close to their usage in everyday life. The cross having a negative connotation corresponds to "incorrect", and hence is used to cancel a menu choice. The circle corresponds to the positive connotation "good" or "satisfactory", and is used to confirm a choice ("OK").

Oddly enough, this meaning, which is not necessarily obvious to westerners, was lost with the localization[123] of some games. Indeed in some North American and European games, both the cross and the circle are used to validate while the square or the triangle are used to cancel. We even find games like Xenogears (1998) that let you cancel an action by pressing on the circle, which is the exact opposite of the Japanese meaning!

Back then, the choice of symbols was no foregone conclusion, but players got used to them, to the point where the four elements

---

122 - 1up.com, All About the PlayStation 1's Design (2010)

123 - The term localization refers both to the transposition of video games and the linguistic and cultural adapting of games to insure their relevance with respect to the target market.

became almost a second logo for the PlayStation, evidencing the brand-new identity of an innovative console. One way of gauging the success of these symbols is to track the way they are more or less identically reproduced by third party game controller makers. The copiers in South-East Asia show a great deal of imagination in copying these symbols without making exact reproductions of the original elements. They do this notably to avoid intellectual property rights infringements. Among the strategies adopted to look slightly different, as shown in Figure 35, we note the following approaches: the use of incomplete symbols (two sides of a square at right angles, two sides of a triangle); derivative but still identifiable shapes (a triangle split in two parts, two half-circles, four segments of circlets) or with extra elements added on such as arrows over the original symbols.

Apart from Sony, the other game controller makers ultimately did not take their exploration of the symbol idea very far. We may, however, mention Philips with the CD-i pad offering four buttons colored gray and black with signs in the shape of small white squares, and the Pippin joypad, the AppleJack, which had tiny concave or convex dots on each of the four action buttons (from one to four). This last solution is interesting because it was a hybrid between a visual symbol and a physical form that was detectable with the thumb without looking at it.

Analog buttons, turbo and force feedback

While the buttons' appearance or the way of naming them are forms of differentiation that are very obvious to the player, we should also stress the way in which the technologies can also make for more discreet specialization. The engineering principles that we described in Chapter 1 have in fact evolved over time. While most action buttons are switches that cut off an electrical signal in a binary way, during the nineties a new wave of electronic components made it possible to introduce analog buttons into game controllers.

With this engineering solution, the buttons can detect the pressure on them, and hence offer a response directly proportional to it. In other words, it is no longer a matter of pressing ON/OFF, you can dose the action level. Such a feature is particularly useful in racing car games where it is an advantage to be able to accelerate or brake gently. One of the first joypads to include analog buttons was the Namco NeGcon (1994), specially designed for this type of game. To make them perform even better, the analog buttons on that model were even arranged in a dip in order to give greater amplitude to the pressure with the thumbs. On this pad, only the left trigger was analog, being used to dose acceleration and braking.

Despite the obvious usefulness of this feature, these analog buttons never really caught on[124]. On Move, Richard Marks, in charge of research and development on this peripheral at Sony, described the value of such a possibility as follows: "It has this analog trigger which really is a great metaphor for squeezing and grabbing. So you can grab and you can put as much pressure as you want to grab something with, which is really great for picking things up or for giving you the ability to just interact with the scene in a way that's completely different than we've been able to do before.[125]" For all the obvious value described in this quote, the fact that they never caught on shows how this technology remained a controversial choice within design teams.

Apart from analog buttons, there is a second type of specialized button based on an engineering solution: the "turbo" button. These buttons correspond to the addition of an electronic component with which to increase (or decrease) the speed of presses on the corresponding buttons. On one of the first joypads to feature this solution, the NES Max (1988), pressing turbo button A enabled the same action as the one associated with button A (jumping in Super Mario Bros., 1985) above it, only repeatedly so (regular jumps in Super Mario Bros.) The turbos came in the shape of a switch of some kind. The on/off type was even more cunning in that the user no longer even needed to press the button to obtain the desired ac-

---

124 - We also find them on the SEGA Saturn and Dreamcast triggers, on the GameCube trigger (with a click indicating maximum pressure), on all the buttons on the Sony Dual Shock 2 (2000), on the four action buttons and L2 and R2 buttons on the Dual Shock 3 (2004), the Sixaxis, Move, on the Xbox triggers and action buttons, and on the triggers and two of the four action buttons on the Xbox 360. Lastly, oddly enough on the Wii Classic, the triggers are analog but this feature was dropped for the Wii Classic Pro.

125 - Interview in Joystiq, August 28, 2009.

tion. On the SEGA and NEC consoles of the eighties and nineties, this was a feature typically used in shoot'em ups to produce steady fire. In arcade games like Street Fighter II (1993), the turbo could also be used to obtain special attacks, and in first person shooter (FPS) games, they served to obtain extremely rapid fire.

These buttons, which were never very popular, have now been abandoned; they featured on various joypads from NEC (PC Engine, Coregafx, Supergrafx and PC-FX) and on the Nintendo NES Max pad, and were also produced by other third party game controller makers (Hori, Gravis, Intec).

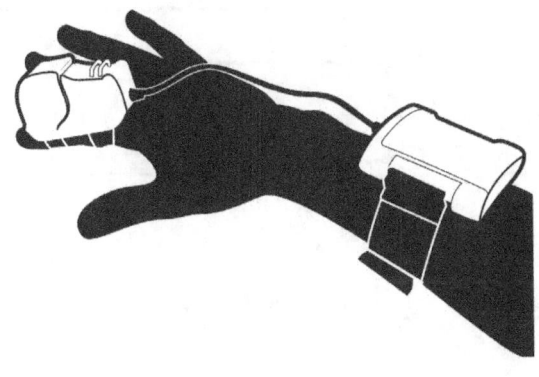

Figure 35: Ore Commander (Hori)

The existence and use of these turbo buttons are interesting because they raise the issue of cheating. With a device like this, does a game not become easier? And most of all, in a game with several players, is it fair to use the turbo? Since it gives players using these buttons an edge by reducing their effort to a minimum, many took the view that it was cheating. This led to a great deal of quarrelling in users' homes over whether this item was a good thing or not. Debates on player forums show that few agree to its being used in this way, so much so that professional player leagues such as the defunct Championship Gaming Series would ban the use of turbo/auto fire buttons as well as the game controllers that offered these interfacing features! Having said that, the manufacturers do not have such a cut-and-dried opinion on this issue. Stephen Toulouse of the Microsoft Enforcement Team described for instance how the use of the turbo buttons was not viewed as cheating and that players using them would not be banned from Xbox LIVE. He also said that it was the job of the video game developers themselves to define what could be done or what was acceptable.

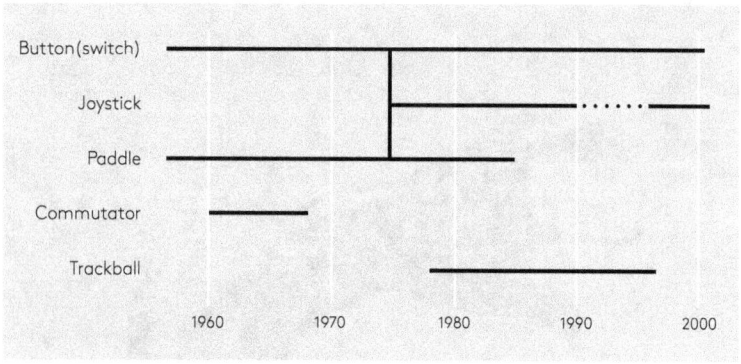

Figure 36: Geneology of button evolution

Having said that, and this is something not often described, console users with neuromuscular conditions that prevent them from repeatedly pressing buttons are a legitimate market for turbo buttons, an interface that allows them to play games that would otherwise be too hard for them.

Lastly, one final, very rare technical possibility involves including a force feedback in the actual buttons, and not in the game controller. This is what you get with a gamepad like the HKS Racing, with a brake or accelerate button carrying this feature. This way the player can feel the weight of the vehicle directly under their thumbs, thereby increasing their immersion in the race.

Revamping, increase and customization

The turbo buttons just discussed are also interesting because they are not always present on the original game controllers. Sometimes they are added on by do-it-yourself players who open up the pad and weld on an extra component. For this to be going on is evidence of the way users of engineering products take them over and alter them through various means. Oddly enough, such practices seem to have grown especially in connection with action buttons. Maybe this is because they are easier to modify, as compared with the direction pad or analog sticks.

From the standpoint of users and game designers alike, the revamping of hardware as designed by the makers is a driving force for ongoing innovation and creative research. One of the most conspicuous examples of this approach is what is known as "button mashing". This, the most basic form of adapting the joypad, requires no special interface as it involves setting the pad on a flat surface or on whatever is to hand and frantically pressing the desired buttons with one or more fingers placed above them, generally the index or middle finger. This practice only involves the action buttons on the front of the joypad, and not the trigger buttons, notably because of the posture you would need to adopt in order to press them quickly. It was arcade players who first developed this way of pressing action buttons at high speed to optimize their performance. Newcomers to these games soon followed suit, pressing randomly as fast as they could, taking it as a way of succeeding in their actions without thinking. Later on, game designers turned it into a design feature. Think for instance of the Track and Field (1983) sports game, which required players to press repeatedly to perform the various athletics events (triple jump, 100 meters, javelin). Subsequently, all games involving repetitive actions (punching, kicking or shooting with action buttons), or moving around (with the d-pad) caught the attention of the "button mashers" as players interested in hammering away at the buttons came to be called.

This way of using the pad is hard to keep up for any length of time, and can be helped along with various items, notably by rubbing a piece of cloth (shirt or tee-shirt) over the buttons, by pressing on them with a spoon or pen, or wrapping elastic bands around the object. With some games that do not call for the direction pad to be operated, the pad can even be set upside down (with the Dual Shock wings pointing up) to make it easier to press the buttons. While button mashing was a must for certain video games, it has also become one way of performing "speedruns", a competition aimed at finishing a game level as quickly as possible.

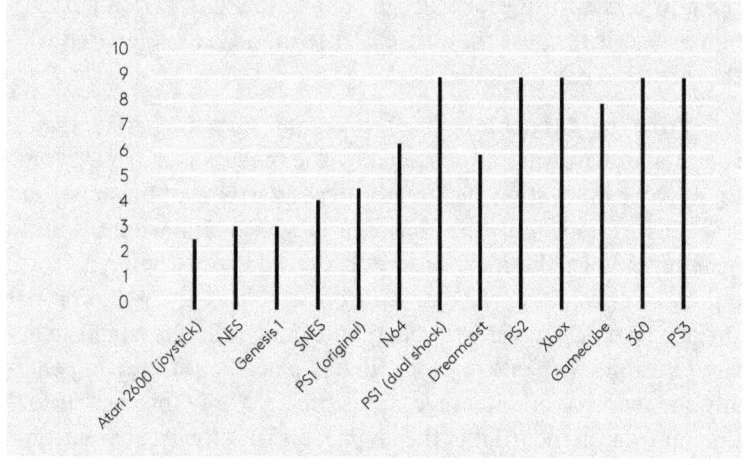

Figure 37: Graphic representation of the highest "Controller Dimensionality" values on the different consoles (after Bateman and Boone, 2006).

However, for really skilled players, button mashing is a frustrating practice, as it is seen basically as no more than a racing performance. In the last fifteen years or so, game designers have moved on and take the view that it is a useful method only now and again in certain gaming situations, such as in an action moment in an adventure game, or in given situations for sports simulation games. But random operation of pads fitted with motion sensors such as the Wii and Move offers a revival of this practice. This is known as the "Wii waggle", when the whole game controller is frantically waggled instead of just the buttons.

Now, as often happens in the history of such techniques, whenever users use an object for some unforeseen purpose, new products are designed to do just that. In particular, the "Ore commander" produced by the gaming peripheral maker Hori, was a gadget purpose-built for button mashing. It is fitted onto the thumb or index finger and is an aid to faster pressing of the action or trigger buttons. A tiny motor inside the piece produces a steady vibration that rapidly moves the thumb for machine-enhanced button mashing.

Less of a caricature is the "N-Control" designed by the Avenger brand. This is an accessory intended to make for more fluid manipulation of the pad buttons. It comprises a shell over the pad of a Dual Shock 3 (or an Xbox 360 pad) and a set of small plastic levers the base of which rests on the action buttons and with the end placed over the triggers. The principle involves enabling players never to lift their thumbs from the analog sticks to change or reload weapons. These actions are performed with the index and middle fingers which, as they lift off the triggers, will operate the levers and thereby press the corresponding buttons. With this accessory, pressing the action buttons becomes indirect and entirely controlled by the index and middle fingers.

Lastly, button mashing enthusiasts can always practice with the Shooting Watch from Hudson Soft (also available in an iPhone version). This is an electronic appliance the same size as a Game & Watch and with it you can count the maximum repeated pressing speed on the buttons. Having only A, B, select and start buttons with an LCD screen for a counter, this apparatus can be considered to be an ultra-minimal video game interface. But it is the appliance designed following on from the Hudson Soft mascot Takahashi Meijin, and it reaches 16 PPS (presses per second).

While button mashing is a major way in which action buttons have been diverted from their intended purpose by players and game designers alike, the possibilities for customizing the actual buttons should also be highlighted. The most conventional form of this involves parameterizing the controls in games. Here you assign some particular function to a button before starting a game. In this connection, researchers who found that this type of customization remained limited in scope proposed to take it further and provide players with a way of physically reshuffling pad components, in particular the action buttons. Players could then choose which elements to use, where to put them and what combinations or "bindings" to use, either before playing or during a game.

In the wake of this type of research, peripheral makers latched onto this new opportunity and brought out game controllers of this type. The Radica Phoenix Revolution is one such; it comes in the form of a standard-shaped wing grip housing on which there are several openings in which to place the analog sticks, the direction pad and the action buttons. Unfortunately, you cannot move the individual buttons, so it falls short of the research. The Valve video game studio also filed a patent for a reconfigurable peripheral that was potentially relevant for some of the games they were bringing out. Although the end result may look rough and ready, and not so neat as a standard joypad, this is an interesting approach, because it can facilitate access to an interface possibly too complicated for beginners. It may also be better suited to certain gameplays, or help to adapt the configuration to players' physical and cognitive skills. For instant, the Access Controller pad produced by eDimensional is intended for one-armed users; the interface elements can be arranged for satisfactory single-handed operation, thereby overcoming their handicap.

Extension of the range of action

Ever since 1983 and the first Famicom joypad, we see how the evolution of action buttons is toward an increase in their presence on game controllers. As we have seen in this chapter, from fast inflation up until the mid-nineties, its growth has leveled off with the following standard features: a practically fixed number, functional specialization (menu and action buttons) and ergonomic specialization (buttons on the front, shoulder buttons and triggers). Combined with the stabilized pad shape and navigation interfaces, namely the direction pad and analog sticks, this evolution ends up with the standard format game controller. It is the model of the Sony Dual Shock, the Xbox 360 joypads and the Wii U Pro peripherals.

In addition, this increase in the number of buttons reflects the creative search for solutions to position the buttons effectively for players without adding extra volume. Given that game controllers have not gotten that much bigger over time[126], it was important to find ways of positioning these interfacing elements without the need for a larger housing. This is one of the reasons for the ergonomic specialization introduced with triggers and shoulder buttons.

Note also how the description of the action interfaces presented in this chapter has been restricted to the buttons. On game controllers comprising motion sensors, actions may be performable through gestures, in addition to what we described on this subject in the previous chapter.

Above and beyond the background to action buttons, what does this description tell us about video games? As in the previous chapter devoted to navigation interfaces, let us remember how the evolution of gaming peripherals reflects the intentions of the game designers behind these game controllers: a "script" corresponding to the actions that they have provided for users to perform. The presence of these buttons, their position and their role in the games can then be understood as concrete form being given to players' ability to act.

To put it another way, to each of these buttons there is a corresponding action verb referring back to what the player can perform on the screen[127]: jumping, shooting, running, opening, etc. In MMI, the word to describe the relationship between an interface, such as a button, and its effect within the computer program is "mapping". The good quality of this correspondence comes from the degree of similarity between the two; for example, a temperature control interface enabling a cursor to be moved up to increase the temperature, and down to lower it, is viewed as relevant. When the physical action somehow mimics the action viewed on the screen,

---

126 - Their size being limited to what can be held in the hands and operated with the thumbs.

127 - Game designers like Chris Crawford moreover propose an action verb definition phase as being a prerequisite for designing a video game and its constituent parts (level, characters, etc.).

Design recommandations

The design recommendations very often obey general ergonomic principles, valid both for the game controller interface and for what is displayed on the screen. They can serve
either as a basis for assessing existing games or as a starting point for games under development. We may quote the
following elements for instance1:

• Consistency: within a game, any one button should have
just one function, and not change roles during a game.

• Standard: in some kinds of games, each button is associated with a standard function that must not be changed,
at the risk of confusing the players.

• Stress: it is preferable to minimize physical stress notably
caused by repeatedly pressing buttons. Hence the need to
avoid having button mashing phases too close together.

• Feedback: utilization of an interfacing element must produce a visible and understandable effect for the player, and
not lead to frustration or incomprehension.

• Simplicity: it is preferable to limit the number of actions to
be performed in order to achieve a single target.

• Versatility: offer shortcuts for experienced players (e.g.
with combinations of buttons) and ways of configuring personally (allocation of actions specific to each button).

However, these recommendations must not be seen as being absolute, notably because the purpose of video games
is to entertain, and it may be appropriate to render an interaction to create a relevant challenge for players. This is
why game design relies on a notion of balance between the
designers' intentions, the technical or interfacing possibilities and players' skills.

this is known as "direct manipulation". This correspondence lets you create the illusion of a physical intervention (pressing a button) having an effect on the digital world. Unfortunately it is not always easy to offer such a direct relationship between an action on the screen and the utilization of an interface. This is what makes all the difference between using a button to hit a tennis ball, and the gesture performed with a Wiimote. In the former case, the correspondence between the two is purely arbitrary and abstract, while in the latter it is more direct.

The evolution of buttons as described in this chapter shows the way the repertoire of actions has increased in complexity over time. Slowly changing over the last thirty years, joypad configuration enabled game designers to offer various options in the definition of performable actions, an important stage in game design[128].

Generally speaking, the first question raised is to do with the choice of buttons to be used in the game that has been devised. This means that the designers can choose to use only a limited number of them. As a rule, this choice is between the buttons present on the console pad, or, in the case of a new peripheral being designed, by adding on new buttons. While the former instance is commoner for game designers who have to make do with the existing pad, the latter is conceivable among console makers and peripheral manufacturers also involved in game design. In all cases, the action buttons, in increasing numbers which have now leveled off, are based on standards with which players are now familiar and which are seldom ignored. Depending on the game type (car racing, first person shooting), the correspondence between the buttons and their effects on the screen is thus highly stereotyped, and few game designers wander off the beaten track.

This choice of the number of buttons involved in a game is obviously highly variable. It depends both on the type of game on offer, on the machine's technical capabilities, and most of all on the target audience – the general rule being, unsurprisingly, that the more you are dealing with occasional and inexperienced users, the fewer buttons there should be. The lower threshold seems to be

128 - In game designer's jargon, the phrase "coding scheme" is used to refer to the definition of the control mode in the game.

the presence of a single button[129]; this is what we find in certain shoot'em up games with horizontal scrolling, where pressing the button is used to lift a ship up in space. More recently, WarioWare Twisted (2004) has been offering several mini-games controllable with a single button. Alongside these instances of games in which the extremely simplified interface is only occasionally used, we should also mention games calling for repeated pressing, as in the defunct sports simulation Track & Field (1983) in its day. Console or computer games with a single button have nonetheless been coming back into fashion in the last few years, notably on cell phones, or in the sphere of freelance developers, who can then take a constraint like this as a creative challenge opening up new opportunities[130].

Another way of defining the utilization of the action buttons involves making it possible to use them in combination with each other. Two cases come to mind here: pressing two or three buttons simultaneously, or pressing buttons in quick succession. This second procedure is a common feature of "combos" of fighting games like Street Fighter. Naturally, this choice implies a degree of complexity, and hence a learning curve for players. So it is more a solution used for games intended for expert players. One variant on the other hand involves repeatedly pressing the same button, either to produce a different effect, or to emphasize the current action. Such an approach thus implies the "button mashing" technique mentioned earlier.

The presence of analog buttons on the joypad can also provide a third way of defining possible actions. For the game designers can now choose to allow the player to dose the intensity of the action to be performed. In a sports game like DOA: Beach Volleyball (2003), the speed of the ball is proportional to the pressure on the button.

Lastly, and this is an uncommon, but potentially creative option, buttons can be made to be operated by different players. Think for instance of the game Klonoa Beach Volley (2002) for two players on a single Dual Shock pad, each taking one side (direction

---

129 - Under which we may wonder whether the title in question is really a video game at all. With no interaction available to the player, it is more like a digital film or artwork.

130 - See inter alia the competition organize by the Kokoromi group.

pad or action buttons). Such a principle relies on the symmetry of the buttons on the PlayStation pads: both the d-pad and the action buttons being distributed in fours in a diamond shape, both players have the same interfacing elements that can be operated on the game controller placed on some support. With Kuri Kuri Mix (2001), one mode works on similar lines: two players control one character and so need to be coordinated to move it around the game world.

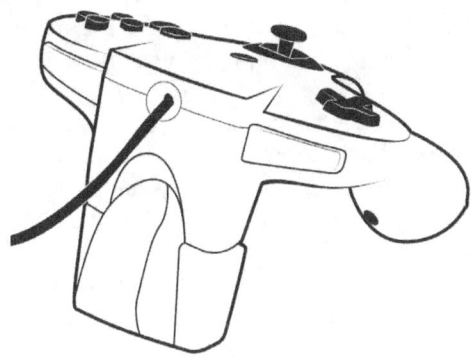

Figure 38: N64 Rumble Pak

The design choices we have just briefly presented imply a balance in order to give the players sufficient freedom while continuing to cater for their habits and to their physical or cognitive skills. Despite numerous tests carried out by the development studios, there is no miracle recipe to insure that the optimal choice of interface is made. There are however some safety barriers, in the form of recommendations[131].

---

131 - See for example Ernest Adams, **Fundamentals of Game Design**, Prentice Hall, 2006.

Controller Dimensionality

Apart from the game type and player profiles, the maximum number of buttons to be used will obviously depend on the game controller and the console for which the game is intended. Designers sometimes use dedicated indicators to assess the difficulty of these choices. Activision in particular resorts to "Controller dimensionality"[1] (CD) by making the following calculation: any movement through two dimensions (from left to right) scores one point, two points in four dimensions (left/right, up/down), with any additional movement (acceleration, sideways movement, braking) worth one point, and any action half a point. On this scale Tetris (1984) has a CD of 1.5 (one point for moving the brick and half a point for rotating it), while Half-Life (1998) scores seven (movements through two dimensions, two-dimensional camera control, extra swimming movement and four types of actions).

The kind of calculation lets you visualize the designers' choices on the various consoles, as shown in Figure 39. A graph like this indicates how games have gradually become more complex over time. The game designers at Activision use this type of indicator to assess the difficulty of their proposed interfaces. When they make this calculation on a game under development, they compare the result with other games of the same type and with a similar audience, notably in order to check on the possible need to reduce the number of available actions.

Part 5 - Incorporation

An ergonomic housing, direction pad, analog sticks, action buttons, triggers, motion sensors… a game controller is composed of all these building blocks fitted together. But the evolution of the joypad does not stop with these components, as designers have included other elements as well. Some of these were intended as novel additional features, others designed to enhance user-friendliness.

This chapter describes this process of gradual incorporation and presents a number of changes made to game controllers at some specific stage. While these changes are not so obvious as their evolving shape, or the advent of interfaces as specific as the direction pad, they have also played a part in setting joypads on their current path.

Feedback in game controllers

The main purpose of the game controller is to act as an input interface to control the game on the screen. But in addition to this conventional role, a number of models can also send back information to the user. This is known as "feedback", referring to the feedback effect of an action on the peripheral that gave rise to it.

Joypad vibrations, or "rumble", in response to players' actions, are the commonest type. This is known as "haptic feedback"[132] as it is felt by the hands holding the pad. The N64 game controller was the first to offer this feature through a small add-on connected to the memory board medium. The device was called the "Rumble pak" and was released in 1997 with the game Starfox 64 (1997). It had a tiny motor operated by two AAA batteries very similar to the motors used in those days to operate pagers. The controller would start to vibrate in reaction to certain phases of a game or would inform the user of the danger of specific situations, notably when they were being followed by an enemy. Note however that ever since the seventies numerous MMI research projects have also addressed the design of feedback interfaces to

132 - From the Greek "haptikos" designating the sense of touch.

obtain a better simulation of the sense of touch with digital interfaces. The joypad's rumble feature is a commercial extension of this work. Similarly, games like Moto-Cross (1976) were already producing a comparable effect on the motorbike handlebars on the arcade machine.

After the Rumble Pak on the N64, third party manufacturers began making similar, less energy-hungry accessories. One such was the Tremor Pack, which could be powered through the game controller itself without the need for batteries. Also, the intensity of the vibrations could be adjusted on the Nyko Hyper Pak Plus, so as to vary this haptic immersion. On the PlayStation, this feature appeared on the Dual Analog pad as of April 1997, with two motors placed under analog sticks. This game controller did not require batteries either, and the presence of two motors was supposed to make for extra immersion. After that, the system was also used on other game controllers, the Dreamcast ("Jump Pack" or "Puru Puru pack" in Japan), on the XBox, the Dual Shock 2 and the Wiimote. Oddly enough, Sony's Sixaxis gamepad did not have this feature, hence its lighter weight compared with earlier versions. According to its designers at Sony, this absence was due to the fact that the vibrations might have interfered with the motion sensor present in the joypad; this seems unlikely since the next model, the Dual Shock 3, has both the sensors and two motors to provide haptic feedback. It would seem that the absence of vibrations on the Sixaxis model was more to do with the litigation that had taken place between Sony and Immersion. This corporation, the owner of patents on such a feature, took the Japanese company to court for borrowing their technology without paying any licence fees.

The rumble was intended to increase immersion in the game, helping the gameplay along in various ways: for instance by creating a special atmosphere, as is the case with Silent Hill 2 (2001), in which the joypad vibrated when the character's heartbeat was racing. In Madden NFL (1998), the use of vibrations intensified the outcome of an action as when the character was hit, or upon explosions in Starfox 64 (1997). The rumble could also be triggered to warn the user of the death of someone nearby in The Sims 2 (2004), or be used as a gameplay in some special way. In The

Legend of Zelda: Ocarina of Time (1998), the joypad would start to shake whenever the player had a certain item (the stone of agony) and was located in certain specific game areas. Likewise, in Metal Gear Solid (1998), the player could use it to detect the presence of antipersonnel mines, by feeling through the joypad how close and intense the vibrations were.

Apart from this haptic feedback, a second feedback mode is featured in some joypad models: sound feedback with the inclusion of a loudspeaker in the device. Despite the obvious value of such an interface, sound is a feedback element we seldom find used in game controllers. It is common on the Wiimote but ultimately had very few predecessors. The 3DO console in 1993 had no speaker but did have a half-hearted sort of audio output, with volume control, to which earphones could be connected to spare anyone nearby. Moreover, the hardware manufacturer Nyko registered interest in 2004, as evidenced by a corresponding patent[133]. While it covered the release of the early versions of the Wiimote for the Wii, the wing grip joypad planned back then was not marketed.

Hence it was the Wiimote that innovated in 2006 with one of the first console game controllers to include a loudspeaker, and to offer various uses of it in different games. Sound feedback in the control peripheral is interesting first from the immersion point of view. The sound of tennis balls, synchronized with the pad vibration, indeed injects a certain amount of realism into games with Wii Sport (2006). Similarly, in The Legend of Zelda: Twilight Princess (2006), the loudspeaker sends back various different sounds depending on the weapons (sword, bow, fishing rod) being used. In this connection, the sound of pulling the bowstring taut is especially evocative, as is the whistling sound as the arrow is fired. Likewise, the death rattle of a dying character in a game like Ju-on: The Grudge (2009), is also an interesting way of reinforcing the impression of getting up close to the characters.

Nonetheless, inserting the speaker in the Wiimote is not just a matter of sound feedback; it also enables some original

---

133 - U.S. patent #6881147: Video game controller with integrated microphone and speaker.

gameplays. Think for instance of games in which sound effects are used to warn the player. In Mario Kart Wii (2008), they are used to indicate that a shell is racing towards one of the participants. In the tutorial and the lower levels of Super Mario Galaxy (2007), there are sounds to indicate when the user needs to shake the Wiimote, point it at the screen, and perform specific actions, or to encourage the player to find something in the scene. This speaker can also be used to enable individual interaction with the player holding the game controller. Thus, in No More Heroes (2007) or Silent Hill (2010), the user can receive phone calls and listen to them by holding the Wiimote next to their ear. This is no longer just feedback, it was for the designers a way of heightening the immersion in the game world by taking care over details that players find important. For example, again in Silent Hill, you can hear the sound of a key hidden in a can when you shake the Wiimote. These uses of the speaker are interesting for the way they show how a multichannel "surround" sound can be obtained fairly cheaply.

Lastly, currently the most popular feedback mode is visual feedback, notably on the Wii U with a screen actually built into the peripheral. If we look at pad evolution, we see however that this option has a number of ancestors. One early, very simple visual feedback option involved adding light emitting diodes (LEDs). The most rudimentary utilization of this feature is to indicate that the console is switched on, either with a single LED (Sony Dual Shocks) or by creating a kind of light halo around the game controller's transparent housing. This is the choice taken for the "Afterglow" range from the Performance Designed Products brand for the Wii, PS2, PS3 and Xbox 360, or their "Tron" model. This is made up of lines of light intended to recall the world of the eponymous science-fiction movie. Certain Alienware brand models are rather subtler and the light comes on when the pad vibrates, thereby adding to the sense of immersion through a visual signal.

More elaborately, HKS from Hong Kong and the Californian Eagle 3 have come up with another way of integrating a screen on the gamepad with the HKS Racing Controller. Designed for car racing games, this controller has a liquid crystal display in the middle informing the player of his speed in the game Need for speed (1994). It comes in the form of digits and a luminous dial.

Figure 39: HKS Racing Controller

Few brands however use these LEDs to provide any more complex information. An earlier game controller model afforded more possibilities: that of the Dreamcast and its VMU (Visual Memory Unit). This was more than just visual feedback, it was a real backup monitor. Broadly speaking, it was the only device of its kind as it was a cross between three appliances: a removable connectible memory chip in the pad (like the memory cards on the N64), a small LCD display[134], and a game controller per se since it had a direction pad and four buttons. The VMU also came with a speaker, an item only found on very recent game controllers like the Wii's. This portable mini-console had a role both as a memory card and the secondary display device for certain games. In multi-user sports games like Ready 2 Rumble (1999), the small screen inserted in the pad displayed statistics that gave a competitive edge over whomever one was playing against. Similarly, in Resident Evil 2 (1998), Resident Evil 3 (1999) and Resident Evil Code: Veronica (2000), the VMU monitor indicated the character's energy gauge, without having to go and look up this information in the dedicated menu on the TV screen. Sometimes the VMU played a further role. In the Sonic Adventures (1998) series, bonuses in the shape of eggs won in the mini-game Chaos Adventure (1998) on the VMU could be transferred to the main game in order to enhance the character's performance.

134 - Displaying 48x32 points in black and white.

You could also connect two VMUs together to share saved games, content reserved for that interface, or mini-games. Finally, this apparatus could also be used as a self-standing portable console, offering with Virtual Tennis (1999) a replica of tennis matches. So you could play without looking at the TV, which prefigures the gameplays available on the Wii U.

Similarly, in 1999 Sony brought out the PocketStation, a miniature personal assistant comprising a black and white LCD screen, a flash memory medium, a speaker and an infrared connection. Unlike the Dreamcast and its VMU, this device was connected directly into the console at the slot reserved for memory cards, and

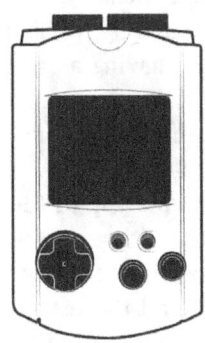

Figure 40: VMU

not to the game controller. The SNK designers have also looked at this type of interaction between the console and a portable apparatus by allowing the Neo Geo Pocket to be connected to the Dreamcast; Nintendo's did likewise by connecting the Game Boy Advance to the GameCube. In the multi-player mode of Final Fantasy: Crystal Chronicles (2003), this configuration enabled each of the participants to view different elements: the map of the current level (player 1), the presence of enemies represented by crosses (player 2), the position of treasures (player 3), or statistics about enemies (player 4). The elements represented on the screen of each GBA changed from one level to the next, making for greater diversity in gameplays. At Nintendo, this utilization of the portable console as a game controller is interesting because the definition on the screen was better than on the VMU at the time. This again is a one-off attempt close to what the Wii U is today.

In the new Nintendo console released in November 2012, the game controller does include a monitor. Its dimensions are in fact more like a cross between a tablet and a joypad since the LCD display occupies nearly half of the surface of the appliance. To understand this product, it is interesting to track back and understand how the Wii designers analyzed how people took to this console. Katsuya Eguchi, head of the Nintendo Entertainment and Analysis Division, combining the former R&D1 and 2 departments, wrote this: "After the Wii was released we kind of watched the patterns of play – how families and friends were playing with the system. We noticed that in the beginning, when it's fresh and new, everyone's getting involved and having a great time, but after a while people get tired of playing the same games all the time. And gradually people started moving away from actually interacting with their Wiis. We noticed that one of the obstacles to getting them to play again was actually having to turn the TV on, then turning the Wii on, and then waiting a while before actually getting in and being able to engage in the activity. When creating the Wii U we wanted to eliminate all those obstacles and also eliminate another obstacle, which was not being able to play while someone was watching TV. So that's where the screen on the new controller came from.[135]"

The solution devised by Eguchi's team was then build a screen into the game controller. The idea was not to offer players an interface to replace the analog stick, but rather to enable novel gameplays through a removable window onto the world to be explored: "That feeling of looking through a screen or a window and having your movements affect what's on that screen is something I don't think people have experienced before.[136]", said Eguchi. By pivoting the controller and its screen, the user can view what is happening above, below or to either side of the scene as shown on the TV screen. Such an approach is basically very similar to certain GBA or 3DS games with Starfox 64 3DS (2011)... which enabled

135 - Interview in Edge #230 (August 2011).
136 - Ibid.

the body to be used as an interface to navigate within the space of the game.

The relationship to projects for a portable console connected to the consoles is an interesting one and it highlights the fact that the production of the Wii U game controller is more than just an opportunistic stroke aimed at cashing in on the extension of the tablet market. On this subject, Eguchi set out the difference between tablets and the Wii U: "Tablets are mainly for one user – they're a very personal thing: one tablet, one user. But our goal for Wii U is for it to be in the living room, where multiple people often enjoy watching TV, and this new controller is intended to change that, to change how people interact with TV, interact with games, and interact with each other. So I'm hoping it won't just be a personal item like a tablet computer.[137]" The example that he put forward at the time is interesting from a gameplay standpoint, although it is fairly conservative in its view of women! The video-conference feature made possible with the screen is thus available with this peripheral and opens up some original possibilities.

Notice also how at the time of designing the Wii a few years earlier, the addition of a touch screen had already come up for discussion. In the Iwata Asks series of interviews, Genyo Takeda said: "the DS had a big influence. We kept in mind how we could follow the DS's path. As many people had been predicting, we even considered including a touch panel on the controller and even considered something that's like a PC mouse or track pad in that can be used as a pointing device.[138]"

However, as Katsuya Eguchi notes, including such a large screen in a game controller raises other problems that the design team tried to deal with: "It's heavier than other Wii controllers so we're thinking about long-term use, how long people can hold it, and in what position. If you hold it straight up, you'll get tired more quickly than if it's on your knees, for example. We're looking at the games and software we're producing and trying to figure out what is the best way to position the controller – whether for

---

137 - Ibid.
138 - Interview in the Iwata Asks series.

certain applications it should be on the table, etc.¹³⁹" Moreover, and this is a major difference with current tablets, the Wii U game controller is not "multi-touch"¹⁴⁰ as it only detects a finger or a stylus. The designers on Eguchi's team put forward two arguments in their defense. First, they were seeking to offer maximum precision, which in their opinion would have been difficult with that technology. But this answer does not go far enough and it may be more a desire to have an inexpensive peripheral. This kind of compromise, aimed at not choosing the most advanced technology on cost grounds, is common practice at Nintendo. Secondly, the game designers wanted to offer gameplay experiences for all types of players, including those not accustomed to multi-touch interfaces. It turns out that it was elderly users who tipped the scales in favor of a more accessible mono-touch interface.

Be that as it may, the inclusion of a screen on the game controller, especially with the SEGA VMU, the GBA connection in the GameCube and the Wii U is a noteworthy trend that we see time and again in joypad evolution. In particular, this is because, generally speaking, their design favored interfacing elements that did not need to be looked at so that the player could focus on what is going on on the screen or TV. As we saw in the chapters about the direction pad or the action buttons, pad designers have gone the extra mile to place the buttons in a good position, or to give them shapes that made them directly perceptible by players with their hands. But to break away from this mode of organization makes sense for two reasons. The first reason is that it is a mistake to think that players do nothing but stare at their screen during a game; they can glance down at their pad, across at their playing partners, or at all kinds of things going on around them. Moreover, the inclusion of a screen is what appears to be a rich fresh opportunity for novel gameplays, one that has so far been little explored.

Above and beyond the screen providing feedback to the players, we see clearly how this built-in feature leads to possibilities for intrinsically novel gameplays. In particular the notion of the "as-

---

139 - Interview in Edge #230 (August 2011).

140 - The term multi-touch refers to interfaces operating with several points of contact (notably with several fingers on the iPhone screens). Conversely, so-called "mono-touch" interfaces have a single contact, as with the Nintendo DS stylus.

symmetric gameplay", as it is called, seems a very attractive one. This term refers to the following idea featured on the Dreamcast VMU: with an auxiliary monitor, one or more players can access a game experience that is distinct from that of their partners. It may be either access to exclusive information, or hidden items, or the possibility of viewing different spaces (by rotating the Wii U through 360 degrees to see what is going on overhead perhaps), or to give the player with the extra screen different skills and objects (firing arrows in The Legend of Zelda: Battle Quest (2012) when the other players can only wield swords). Given that the players do not all have the same view of the gaming space, the gameplay thus becomes "asymmetric". Nintendo's pioneering position in this direction is interesting, and looking at the competition, they certainly seem to be attracted to this technology. In this connection, Sony have also filed a patent for a game controller connected to a screen[141].

Wireless

Several of the early gaming machines connected to a TV set had one feature that nowadays we find rather peculiar: the control interface was originally located inside the actual game console. Various clones of Pong were thus playable directly on the apparatus with the knobs very close to each other. In this connection, the patent filed by Ralph Baer and his colleagues at Sanders[142] shows a similar assembly (Figure 5). Gradually, small detachable boxes fitted with knobs appeared. This is the format that was adopted by the designers of various game controllers during the seventies and early eighties, including the Odyssey by Magnavox, the Atari VCS, the Intellivision and the Vectrex.

With the advent of these control devices as the ancestors of joypads, all kinds of connection issues were raised: how to connect the game controller to the console effectively? What to put in the gamepad and what to leave in the console's CPU? What length of

141 - U.S. patent #20120220278: Information processing system, communication terminal, information processing unit and program.

142 - U.S. patent #RE32282: Television gaming apparatus.

cable should be used? What form of cable to use? The history of game controllers shows in this regard three stages of evolution, taking advantage of the inclusion of the different components in the joypads.

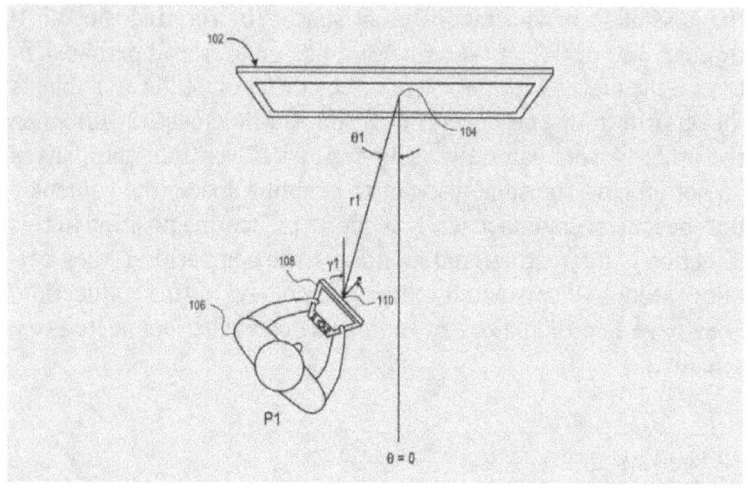

Figure 41: Proposed Sony game controller with screen (Patent No. 20120220278)

The first stage concerns the configuration of the Nintendo Famicom (1983): the gamepads were connected to the console with a cable, but the cable was not detachable. If ever a joypad broke down you had to take the whole console to the repair shop! The reason why the design team decided on this option was the cost issue. As Hiroshi Imanishi, then general manager at Nintendo, recalls: "We really had to be creative in order to lower the console's price [...] The controllers were directly attached to the console without any possibility to unplug them, because it cost less than producing plugs. Similarly, the cables that connect the pads to the console were relatively short so that we could save money.[143]"

When the western version of the Famicom (NES) was designed, the principle of gamepads with a cord that was detachable

143 - Nintendo Dream #95 released in July 2003, cited in Florent Gorges, op. cit.

from the console seemed important. This was stage two of pad evolution. The Nintendo designers were converted to this type of system, and so were their competitors at SEGA, NEC and Atari. Unfortunately, the advent of these long wires brought problems of their own. It is the same old story: someone steps past the console a little too fast, catches their feet in the cord, the game controller is knocked onto the floor and the console falls off the coffee table... And yet this was the standard configuration for gaming consoles, fitted with two to four connectors, which we again find during the nineties. Notice however that there are exceptions, with connector multipliers that were very useful for certain multi-user games, notably Bomberman on PC Engine. Alongside this standard model, the 3DO offered one interesting exception since the joypads were all connectable to each other, offering a "daisy chain" connection with up to eight pads.

The design of wireless game controllers came as a third stage, which appears in hindsight as an adjustment also seen in other appliances. However, despite the existence of remote control radio technologies since the late nineteenth century[144], and their application to the field of television starting in the fifties, it is strange that we have had to wait so long for gamepads to get the benefit of this. The delay is due to the fact that video games called for continuous communication between the game controller and the monitor, and not a single press intended to change channels or control the volume.

The earliest gamepads using this technology date back to the eighties. A prototype of an Atari console called 2700 and designed by Roy Nishi had two wireless joysticks. But owing to two major technical problems, the device was never marketed. On the one hand, the controllers were recognized by each console with a unique identifier; which means that if ever one of the joysticks malfunctioned, you could not use the console with a different model! A second problem arose from the interferences that these two boxes had on radio-controlled devices located within a radius of 300 meters around the joysticks.

---

144 - U.S. patent #0,613,809: Method of and Apparatus for Controlling Mechanism of Moving Vehicle or Vehicles.

With the Atari CX-42 (1982), the first wireless pad model to come on the market, the game controllers used the same frequency as the remote controls opening garage doors, and sent the signal to a transmitter connected to the console. With these pads you could play while holding the joystick some 20-30 feet away, but the appliance was very bulky and hard to hold in the hands, on account of the presence of the emitter and a 9-volt battery. Apart from these issues of bulkiness, there was often a delayed response to commands made by the player with the stick; not to mention the fact that operating the game controller would sometimes accidentally open the garage door.

With the evolution of joypads in the eighties and nineties the steady increase in the number of buttons and interfacing elements in game controllers also placed a limit on the use of wireless technology. This is because the radio waves previously employed were not suitable for the increasing complexity of these pads. That is why developers turned to another technology regularly used in televisions and VCRs: infrared transmission. This was the case with the NES Satellite and the SEGA MK-1646-50 model II for the Mega Drive. This technology did not have the disadvantage of activating other household appliances, and operated at greater distances between the game controller and the console, since players could be seated up to about twenty-three feet away from the TV. But the infrared waves did have one major drawback: to use them you had to point the gamepad directly at the receiver on the console. Anything coming between the two was liable to cause a loss of signal and hence have an influence on the game in progress. So there were problems whenever a person or pet passed in front or even when the gamepad wobbled. Likewise, the infrared data transmission was mono-directional, meaning that the console could not send vibratory-type feedback (rumble) to joypads with the force feedback feature.

For all the above reasons, these infrared game controller models met with no great commercial success, and pad designers once again turned to radio waves with a different frequency range from the models of the eighties; namely between 902 and 928 MHz for these new models such as AirPlay (produced by a third party maker for the PlayStation). Technical advances enabled these to operate without continuously pointing the game controller directly at the receiver, and could also emit and receive at the same time, thereby enabling the rumble function. In addition, this return to radiofrequencies also enabled a maximum four wireless pads to be used all at once.

In the early years of the new millennium, the advent of the WiFi standard, using the 2.4 GHz frequency band, was seen as an important stage. Unlike the radio waves used up till then, this new current standard in the electronics industry was interesting because it required less energy, enabled more data to be transmitted, and at a faster rate, thereby solving problems with delayed transmission. Apart from the products of third party manufacturers, it was Nintendo who brought out the first official joypad using the 2.4 Ghz frequency, with the WaveBird Controller[145] designed for the GameCube, but also operating on the Wii. With this latest model, players could be anywhere between 20 and 60 feet away from the receiver. Following Nintendo's lead, the designers at Microsoft also chose this frequency, utilizing the WiFi communication protocol for the Xbox 360 game controller, while at Sony they focused on the Bluetooth standard[146], using the same frequency for the Sixaxis and the Dual Shock 3. With the Wiimote, Nintendo's designers also converted to Bluetooth, used along with an infrared pointer.

This gradual evolution of wireless technologies shows us how there is no ultimate solution and how designers combine the various possibilities in order to meet players' needs: to avoid having wires getting in the way, to be able to have several people playing together and at a comfortable distance from the screen.

On a less regular basis, over the years various components have been built into game controllers, and then discarded by the designers of the models that followed.

---

145 - A company in Texas, Anascape, took Nintendo to court for a patent infringement regarding this technology. But Nintendo made a successful appeal and was able to carry on marketing the WaveBird.

146 - Different communication protocols can be used on a single frequency. Bluetooth and WiFi both operate in the 2.4 Ghz range but have a different way of encoding the information.

Among these, memory chips have an interesting place, albeit limited to a few joypad models. Given the impossibility of storing information on the game itself in the case of devices fitted with CD-ROM players (as opposed to cartridges), these devices were frequently used as a way of saving a game and other gaming elements such as characters' characteristics. Starting in the early nineties, such integration could be found on the Neo Geo (SNK), the TurboGrafx (NEC) and the Mega-CD (SEGA). Before becoming standard features directly in the console, several game controller models allowed you to insert a memory chip inside the pad itself. These notably include the N64 Controller Pak (32 Mb) and the Dreamcast VMU (128 Mb). Nintendo's designers did not renew this attempt with the GameCube, on which the chips are connected to the console itself. Conversely, the Wiimote contains a flash memory limited to 6Kb with which to save the player's avatars (Mii)[147], along with the utilization of cards with more space on the CPU.

Keyboards are a second range of items built into certain joypad models. While the early consoles had a keyboard connectable to the device (Famicom), some inspired designers have attempted to add this interface directly to the game controller. Thus we find mini-keyboards for connecting to the Xbox 360 pad, a GameCube controller-keyboard a foot wide (Sammy), or the mini-keyboards for the Dual-Shock 2 produced by Sony. In each of these cases, the idea was to have the benefit of the richness of the alphanumeric keyboard to act in games, notably role-playing games (RPGs), and thereby offer a dialog interface. Despite the technical challenge that this insertion represented, in practice most of these appliances turn out to be hard to operate. One of the reasons for this is to do with the difficulty keying in from a keyboard when it is not set on a stable support. The combination of a joypad held in both hands and operated with the thumbs, thus seems to be in contradiction with the logic behind using a keyboard. The minikeys positioned on the bottom of the joypad on the Xbox 360 or the Dual Shock 2 get round this problem, but unfortunately they are too small to be used effectively with the thumbs. Only certain skillful players with

---

147 - U.S. patent #4949298: Memory cartridge having a multi-memory controller with memory bank switching capabilities and data processing apparatus.

enough patience to learn how to manipulate these devices enjoy using them.

Apart from the accelerometers, magnetometers etc. built into the Wii or Move, sensors form a third range of items built into joypads. It is at Nintendo that we find the most interesting examples. In particular, on the original Famicom, one of the pads included a microphone. As then Nintendo general manager Hiroshi Imanishi, describes: "The microphone in the second controller was never really used. When designing the console, we thought about voice-controlled game. For instance, talking or screaming in order to fight enemies. We thought it might be useful This idea never really took off, but we tried certain experimentations with it.[148]" This sound sensor enabled the voice to be used as a control interface; in Raids on Bungeling Bay (1984), the player who had the pad with the microphone could control his characters by shouting into the gamepad. In the game Kid Icarus (1986), you could get cut prices whenever the player spoke directly to the dealers in the game world. Singing a karaoke song to advance was another possibility in Takeshi No Chousenjou (1986). Unfortunately, the console's voice recognition capability was poor, and in practice sound interactions proved rather rudimentary. It was more a matter of the Famicom capturing sounds than detecting anything meaningful.

The N64's BioSensor is another example of a sensor built into a joypad. Produced by SETA in 1997 and released in 1998, it was only available in Japan, and was generally sold with the Tetris 64 game. It was connected to the N64 game controller on the extension port in place of the Rumble Pak, and was linked to a clip fixed to the player's ear lobe. This sensor was used to measure the heart rate and adjust the speed of the mini-game Bio-Tetris accordingly: the bricks could thus be speeded up or slowed down depending on the stress level. So this peripheral may be seen as a dry run for Nintendo and their Wii Vitality Sensor. Announced in 2009, the release date was repeatedly postponed for this Wii accessory containing an oxymeter. This was used to detect heartbeats, while measuring the oxygen level in the blood, so as to adjust the game accordingly. However, in 2012 this accessory had still not come onto the market. With their patent on biometric recognition[149], the Sony engineers were meanwhile looking into sensors with which to identify a particular user, and so provide suitable content for that user.

Alongside these physiological sensors, as they are called, detecting changes in the functioning of the human body, we should also note the presence of NFC technology in the Wii U game controller[150]. Already present on cellphones, especially in Japan and in South Korea, this is a radio communication system comparable to WiFi or Bluetooth. But unlike them, NFC requires a very short distance (no more than four inches) between the elements to be brought into contact. With this type of sensor in the pad, the idea is obviously to enable the use of cards (such as Pokemon), or figurines (of the Skylanders type) to pass over the controller in order to modify the action in progress in the game. This solution also allows direct payment on the pad: the player passes his prepaid card over the left face of the gamepad and can use his credits on his Nintendo Network account. Likewise, promotional items might also allow access to original content in some games (bonuses, hidden levels). The combination of cards with console games is also relevant in a cross-media approach, notably with publications (magazines, books) offering a solution in terms of how to link content on different media.

Finally, the oddest item to be built into a pad has got to be the fan present in models like Nyko's AirFlo (2003) or Logitech's ChillStream (2006). They were designed to dry gamers' sweaty hands during long frantic sessions. A one-off insertion in game controllers, they are nonetheless an interesting example of how engineered objects can fill a gap or meet some specific need.

All these elements are interesting as instances of temporary integration in game controller evolution. They evidence the official manufacturers' and third party makers' willingness to experiment, although these models remain no more than sideshows.

---

149 - U.S. patent #20070079137: Process and apparatus for automatically identifying user of consumer electronics.

150 - Stands for "Near Field Communication".

Evolutionary paths

Although this chapter is very dense, and reads like a catalog of items built into game controllers, it brings to light an interesting phenomenon that goes beyond the scope of this book; the inclusion of sensors, a screen or a wireless emitter in joypads is nothing new. This trend is even central to the history of video games accessories, advancing in stages repeated after multiple failures. The example of wireless communication speaks volumes in this regard since it took several generations of consoles and technologies to arrive at a stable, functional system, this despite the fact that the TV remote control was first invented back in the fifties.

Likewise, it should be remembered that the presence of a screen in a game controller is not restricted to the VMU Dreamcast or the Wii U. In fact, the history of portable consoles, from the Game Boy to the PlayStation Vita, could be recounted as that of one branch in the evolution of joypads. Both the actors in this history and the interfaces proposed are very similar to the protagonists of what we have seen. And this is because a portable console is nothing if not a joypad in which the designers have vied with each other to find a way to merge one or more screens, the console and sometimes even its power supply. From an evolutionary point of view, the underlying idea is individuation giving rise to another distinct, integrated item. The game controller having become a standard mode of interaction, there had to be a similar system available for the mobile version. The lack of diverging attempts, apart from electronic games, shows how an analysis of the portable console interfaces would likely evidence a relative dearth in comparison with the broad range of joypads that we have described.

It is also fascinating to note how the insertion of a screen in a game controller, as in the case of the Wii, also demonstrates how ideas do the rounds: the Game & Watch games and later joypads gave rise to a new independent path: the portable console. Portable consoles in return have influenced game controllers, and the design of both the Wii and the Wii U were inspired by the Nintendo DS and the ways it was used. In the "Iwata asks" series, Genyo

Takeda explained how the DS had a big influence[151]. Saying this, he testifies to the way in which the hardware design for the portable console, and the gameplays that it offered, fuelled the design of the Wii and the Wii U, notably by offering a versatile interface that could be used either with the fingers on buttons or a stylus by players of every age. Here again we find something similar to the design of the Famicom game controllers based on the Game & Watch experience.

In addition, this chapter has also shown how the evolution of game controllers is not always obvious, since profound but less perceptible modifications are being made through the insertion of sensors, speakers or radio transmitters. Moreover, we should note how it is precisely the inclusion of new elements of this type that is guiding current developments. We see this with the Wii and Move, and also with the Wii U and the prototypes in the pipeline at Sony or third party makers like Valve. To take this reasoning as far as it will go, we might even say that with Microsoft Kinect, that is the whole story, with the disappearance of the game controller object per se! Sensors, in the shape of a 3D camera, then come to replace the joypad, turning the player's body into a direct interface with what is happening on the screen[152].

As we saw at the end of previous chapters, the overall appearance and interface of joypads as such were globally stabilized in terms of shape and interface. The evolution of game controllers is ultimately not so much to do with key elements like buttons or shape (although the shape can evolve through the inclusion of a screen in the case of the Wii U) as with the integration of less visible components. These then provide extra comfort (no wires), greater immersion (sound feedback), and also some original gaming features (asymmetric gameplay).

---

151 - Interview in the "Iwata Asks" series.

152 - Hence the absence of the game controller in the case of Kinect is the reason why this book has little to say about that technology!

Conclusion

Joypad evolution basically boils down to the individualization of an original control interface, a separate "lineage" in the history of personal computing, alongside keyboards and mice.

This book has brought out this specific, singular path. It may be seen as a gradual combination of existing engineering principles (switches, potentiometers, screen), electronic components (memory chip, sensors, wireless communication transmitters, motors) in a housing whose shape meets certain ergonomic criteria (morphology of the hands, opposable thumbs) and context-sensitive criteria (home environment, resting position on a sofa).

Basic building blocks were initially juxtaposed with more of a do-it-yourself mindset than with the idea of designing a new unit. These were the early days in the research laboratories of North America with the advent of the ancestors of the video game and their control boxes. Over time, this juxtaposition has tended towards integration since each of these elements was combined into a whole that became coherent and unified[153]. It was also at that time, in the years 1989-1990, that interfaces specific to joypads (direction pad, double analog stick, diamond-shape button layout) appeared. The game controllers "associated environment", formed on the basis of the engineering principles available at any given period, game designers' intentions and their designs, and also the players themselves have all had an influence on these design choices. This was the second period with the design of the first consoles then the gamepads as individualized objects, and mostly designed by Japanese electronics manufacturers.

An analysis over the long term such as is proposed here evidences the relative continuity of this item throughout the successive generations of console. Despite technology companies seeking to "revolutionize" the field, we have noted a gradual variation

---

153 - Thus the philosopher of techniques Gilbert Simondon would use the word "concretization" to refer to this coherent evolutionary process. He was going back to the etymology of the term, meaning "that which grows together".

of which presentday joypads are the outcome. Similarly, we have seen how embryonic changes that seem recent (sensors, utilization of physiological data) have featured in gaming peripheral design more or less since the joypad's inception.

The story we have told here shows a convergence and stabilization over its thirty-year existence. Looking at the variety of models in the years 1985 to 2000, we note how the broad range of the early days was followed by a phase of gradual pruning. Like other engineered objects, such as the keyboards on typewriters and computers in the eighties, "various irreversible processes occur at various different stages, thereby narrowing down the field of desired items and desirable practices".[154] These processes lead to the "extinction" of several engineering principles: spherical shapes, trackballs, or the stick screwed onto the direction pad are good examples of this. Irreversibility is such that the most up-to-date pad models, the Xbox 360, Wii U Pro and Dual Shock 3, all look alike and have a set of common features such as the "wing grip", the presence of a d-pad, a double analog stick, the diamond-shaped layout of the action buttons, the existence of triggers, and possible wireless communication with the console.

Each of these features of today's pads corresponds to a key moment in joypad evolution. It might be said that our current game controllers sum up the history of gamepads, as these elements were adopted by designers as being sufficiently relevant to deserve inclusion in later models. The only missing ones are motion sensors and the presence of a screen; they seem to have spawned parallel ranges of gaming peripherals with the Wiimote, Sony Move and Wii U. Notice too how while these modifications have been "circulating", others were one-off happenings: action buttons set in sixes in two rows (Mega Drive and Saturn), a spherical-shaped housing (Saturn), double direction pad (Virtual Boy), trackball (AppleJack) etc.

Lastly, notice the inequality of the different makes in carrying out such innovations. While Sony's designers can take the credit for including the double analog stick or for the advent of "wing grip" handles, and SEGA's are responsible for the rows of buttons

154 - Delphine Gardey, La standardisation d'une pratique technique: la dactylographie (1883-1930), Réseaux, volume 16 #87, 1998.

or analog buttons, top marks go to the designers at Nintendo, to whom we owe the direction pad, the return of analog sticks, vibration in gamepads, shoulder buttons and the diamond-shape layout. So if there is one make offering irreversible changes, it has to be Nintendo. This situation shows the various steps involved in innovation operating at these technology companies. Broadly speaking, while the designers at Nintendo seem to have made the games their main concern, and to have designed their interfaces accordingly, this seems to have been less the case for designers working for Atari, SEGA, NEC, Sony or Microsoft. Taking a more conventional engineering approach, they have focused primarily on designing hardware, without necessarily taking games as a starting point and then devising the equipment to go with them.

On the subject of the corporations, we should also stress the decidedly collective approach to design. Each and every instance of breaking new ground that we have described here contradicts the "myth of the lone inventor" being hyped in many publications from video games enthusiasts, and more generally in the way we talk about "inventions". By double-checking the information gleaned from the biographies of some of the people involved in the story (Gunpei Yokoi for Nintendo, Ken Kutaragi for Sony) against the patents, interviews with designers and third party documents, we have seen how these designs were rarely the handiwork of a single person. The evolution of game controllers, like that of complex engineered objects such as mice, video games or cellphones, is the result of teamwork. And the people involved in innovations like these do not all work in the same field, as we have seen from the Nintendo patents involving industrial designers, hardware engineers and programmers.

Change and irreversibility

To summarize the history of joypads, we need to end with two dynamics that we have seen at work throughout this book: one the dynamic of change, driving designers to propose new models, and the dynamics or irreversibility, which explain why certain choices survive and others fall by the wayside.

Why have we encountered so many different models? What are the motivations behind this constant tinkering? Through the examples presented in this book, we have looked at a number of possible reasons[155]. The presence of numerous types of joypad is understandable first in view of the renewal of peripherals with each new generation of consoles. Like Sony and Microsoft, some makers could have been content to stick with game controllers that were very similar to each other. They have not always done so, as we see with Nintendo and SEGA constantly seeking further enhancements. Technical advances on consoles seems to have played a key role in the production of new models: the availability of faster or more powerful microprocessors, and graphics boards offering closer to photograph quality resolutions and thereby calling for more sensitive controls is one good example of this. Another opportunity for innovation comes from being able to detect players' actions with greater accuracy through buttons and sensors.

Nonetheless, various examples have also shown us how technology has not always come first in making design choices. We have seen on several occasions how game design decisions could spark engineering choices that did not involve the very latest technology. And this has sometimes been due to excessive cost, or to get better performance out of the hardware. As Takashi Tezuka, a game designer with Nintendo, says: "Hardware technology is very important, but if we rely too much on the hardware and not enough on ideas, you won't make games. You'll have demonstration software. New technology can make things more interesting. For example, the Nintendo 64 can produce advanced images, but if that's all we emphasize, the game will be boring. The problem we face is how to use advanced technology to enhance game play. The technology is just a tool for the expression of ideas.[156]" Contrary to conventional wisdom, we have also seen a number of times that video games are not necessarily as advanced as the media claim; obviously they use state-of-the-art 3D technologies, but it was twenty years before effective wireless joypads came in, and

155 - We have left the economic aspect to one side. The driving force behind innovation for the companies mentioned also lies in the logic of capitalist growth: winning over new markets, acquisition, geographical expansion and creating new products.

156 - Interview with Shigeru Miyamoto and Takashi Tezuka, **Nintendo Power** vol. 80, January 1996.

over ten years went by between first utilization of motion sensors in automobile airbags and their introduction in a game controller!

Although it is more readily identified with hindsight[157], irreversibility in joypad evolution is interesting because it raises a fundamental question: what is it about an alteration that means it will be kept on in subsequent models? Our trip down memory lane provides a few indications as to what is going on here. First of all, such interfacing building blocks are kept because they serve some relevant purpose for users. The direction pad made it possible to individualize and concentrate the control of a character's movements on a dedicated interface; the analog stick combined with camera buttons made for intuitive navigation in 3D spaces, and so on. To put it another way, they are effective for the types of games being produced.

To the types of game devised by game designers (platform, first person shooting, 3D navigation, etc.) there are, then, corresponding specific choices regarding the pad that need to be taken into account by companies collectively. A constraint like this explains the convergence towards a standard model, as we find similar styles on all consoles. The functional requirement of being able to control all these games thus led to a kind of single optimum multi-purpose solution. Conversely, makers interested in just one particular type of game (Neo Geo and the arcade game in the nineties, Nintendo and casual games on the Wii) have been able to offer interfaces with a difference while offering a more conventional pad for playing standard games. So we observe makers' different strategies: either stand apart from the competition, or stick to whatever has become the standard. Despite their communication which seems to emphasize the differences, all the same, the major players Nintendo, Sony, Microsoft) all seem to be converging on a single solution since, despite Wii U, Move or Microsoft Kinect, they are all producing conventional joypads for their latest models.

Taking the morphology of the hands into account has been another key factor in the "survival" of interfacing elements. From the moment they were used to control the character on the screen, this opened up a number of possibilities: the presence of a small housing, ergonomic shape for holding comfortably, optimum operation with the thumbs. These different principles had an influence on designers' choices; the parallelipedal box was given a curved shape and gradually adapted to fit better in the hands. Some alternative solutions were tried (N64, Dreamcast, Jaguar), but little by little, the standard wing grip model emerged. Similarly, the d-pad and the current sticks owe their survival partly to their strategic position for operation with the thumbs. This joint presence of both these interfaces dedicated to navigation also shows the object's versatility in providing several different ways of controlling what is happening on the screen, a diversity that offers a variety of gameplays to users with different levels of skill.

Similarly, designing a game controller also involves finding harmony between the interactions that the designers are offering and the surface of the gamepad. The search for the optimum number and positioning of the buttons are evidence of this: too many features (Jaguar) and the item is incomprehensible, while too few buttons means not having all the features you need. So this is the balance that has to be struck and which explains the high density on today's pads and the use of every available space (front, underside, shoulder).

Moreover, the close link between hardware and software design is a further important aspect that has counted in the survival of certain interfacing elements. We may note how the successful gamepad transformations have all been linked to outstanding games: the direction pad designed for Donkey Kong (Game & Watch, 1981), extra buttons added on for porting Street Fighter 2 (1992) on the Mega Drive or Super Famicom, the analog stick design for 3D games and Super Mario 64 (1996) in particular, and so on. Also it would appear that one way of assessing the potential success of a change to the joypad involves observing whether they strike a subtle balance between breaking new ground and continuity with the past. Mutations are relevant and adopted by designers when they do not disturb players too much, while leaving a little leeway for those more open to innovations. So the Sony designers' strategy is interesting in this respect; the advent of the double analog stick was a small step forward between the first two game controllers, and the Sixaxis including a built-in sensor are two good examples of transformations that did not force conservative players to change their habits. Conversely, being too original, pads like the AppleJack and its trackball, just flustered their users.

A future without game controllers?

No book on the history of joypads can end without saying something about their future. Recent trends, especially having no handheld peripheral in the case of Microsoft Kinect, regularly cause some people to fear the worst: might it lead to their possibly disappearing altogether? Everything that has been brought together in this book provides some kind of an answer to this question.

Game controller evolution as we have described it here leads us to think that they still have quite a future before them; first, because they represent an optimal interface for a whole range of games that have already been designed with them in mind. In this regard, they form a straightforward, flexible solution to the whole set of actions offered by the main genres of console video games. And secondly, the corollary of this is that a host of players are used to it, or attached to it. Hence the current standard, with the Dual Shock 3, the Xbox 360 and the Wii U Pro, is particularly settled, like the computer keyboard that has remained unchanged for decades. Like the computer keyboard, the joypad is a common denominator as it is suitable for platform, racing, fighting and adventure games, and games of strategy as well. Despite the obvious attractiveness of gestural interfaces, many players are well aware that the realism and sensitive control of the characters are often best achieved with a gamepad. The complexity of some games moreover calls for a peripheral that offers enough possibilities for interaction with the fewest buttons such as corresponds to the repertoire devised by game designers. Neither 3D cameras nor game controllers fitted with sensors allow the same control for these games. On the other hand, it is interesting to observe the birth of a gaming culture built around these peripherals. Strictly speaking we are no longer talking about video games, which leads directly to tension and scorn from adepts of the "history channel video game"! These people do not find these alternative forms of gaming interesting or even relevant, on account of their mastery of game-pads after many long hours playing with them.

One possible option for joypad evolution may indeed involve the addition of new types of sensors. Among the factors influencing game controller design, the notion of incorporating technologies into pads is definitely the richest today from a forward-looking standpoint. The addition of a built-in and clickable two-point capacitive touch pad on the front of the Dual Shock 4 is obviously a good example of such evolution. If we want to imagine what the future holds for game controllers, we need then to look at what items a pad might include. With the advent of a touch screen, above and beyond the auxiliary screen and asymmetric gameplays, this marks the birth of enhanced reality applications. The screen-controller can then not only represent the digital world, but also visualize the physical space enriched with items superimposed as on mobile phones. Likewise, the presence of NFC-type sensors can run global positioning programs inside the home, with the player having to touch items concealed inside the house. In this connection, observing MMI mockups at research centers or consulting patents filed by manufacturers such as Apple, Microsoft, Nintendo or Valve gives an idea of integrations now in the pipeline. In particular, physiological sensors like the Wii Vitality Sensor, podometers, satnavs and interfaces detecting brain activity all feature on the list.

These various examples show how the evolution of game console peripherals is following the overall current trend in computing with the massive incorporation of information and communication technologies into everyday items. Utilization of NFC in fact takes us in this direction, enabling the gamepad to interact with cards or figurines today, and maybe tomorrow with enhanced phones or books.

Acknowledgements

Nicolas Nova: Emmanuelle Jacques (for introducing me to Gilbert Simondon, Yves Desforges and Quynh Delaunay's history of the washing machine which definitely gave me the idea for this book), David Calvo, Étienne Mineur, Basile Zimmermann for endless discussions on the notion of circulation, Julian Bleecker, Fabien Girardin, Frédéric Kaplan, and Matthieu Pellet for his careful proof-reading, Daniel Sciboz, Pro Helvetia and the Game Culture program, Timothée Jobert for his advice on the historical approach, Patrick Gyger, Marc Atallah and the Maison d'Ailleurs, Claire Favre Maxell and Mudac, John Ikeda, Mike Ambinder.

Laurent Bolli: All the illustrations and photographs were produced by BBStudio - Lausanne, Switzerland founded by Cristiana and Laurent Bolli. My thanks to Gaël Paccard, Gaël Vulliens, Gaël Kilchherr, Fabrice Berger and Sébastien Davila for their numerous graphic contributions. Special thanks to Gaël Paccard for his skills in portable studio photography work.

Bibliography

Ernest Adams, *Fundamentals of Game Design*, Prentice Hall, 2006.

Madeleine Akrich, *"The De-Scription of Technical Objects"*, In Bijker, W.et Law, J., ed, Shaping Technology/Building Society. Studies in Sociotechnical Change, MIT Press, 205-224 (1992).

Reiji Asakura, *Revolutionaries at Sony*, McGraw Hill, 2000.

Georges Basalla, *The Evolution of Technology*, Cambridge Studies in the History of Science, 1989.

Chris Bateman and Richard Boon, *21st Century Game Design*, Charles River Media, 2006.

Wiebe Bijker, *Of bicycles, bakelites and bulbs: Toward a Theory of Sociotechnical Change*, MIT Press, 1995.

Ian Bogost and Nick Montfort, *Racing the Beam: The Atari Video Computer System*, MIT Press, 2009.

Pierre Contensou, *"L'Apport de Robert Esnault-Pelterie"*, L'Aéronautique et l'astronautique, no 97, 1982.

Yves Deforge, *Technologie et génétique de l'objet industriel*, Maloine, 1985.

Tristan Donovan, *Replay: The History of Video Games*, Yellow Ant, 2010.

Delphine Gardey, *"La standardisation d'une pratique technique: la dactylographie (1883-1930)"*, Réseaux, volume 16 n°87, 1998.

Paul M. Fitts, *"The information capacity of the human motor system in controlling the amplitude of movement"*, Journal of Experimental Psychology, Vol. 47(6), 1954.

Florent Gorges, *L'histoire de Nintendo 1980-1991*, l'étonnante invention: les Game & Watch, Editions Pix'n Love, 2009.

Jessie Cameron Herz, *Joystick Nation: How Computer Games Ate Our Quarters, Won Our Hearts and Rewired Our Minds*, Little Brown & Company, 1997.

Osamu Inoue, *Nintendo Magic: Winning The Video Game Wars*, Vertical, 2010.

Hiroshi Ishii and Brygg Ullmer, *"Tangible bits: towards seamless interfaces between people, bits and atoms"*, Proceedings of the SIGCHI97 conference on Human factors in computing systems, 1997

Stephen Jay Gould, *The Panda's Thumb. More Reflections in Natural History*, Norton & Company, 1980.

Steven E. Jones and George K. Thiruvathukal, *Codename revolution: The Nintendo Wii Platform*, MIT Press, 2012.

Graeme K. Kirkpatrick. *Controller, Hand, Screen: Aesthetic Form in the Computer Game*, Games and Culture, No.4, 2009.

Takefumi Makino, *Gunpei Yokoi: vie et philosophie du dieu des jouets*, Nintendo, Editions Pix'n Love, 2011.

Nicolas Nova, and Timothée Jobert, *"Intuitivité et incorporation des interactions gestuelles chez les utilisateurs de jeux vidéo"*, Actes de la conférence IHM09, 2009.

Georges Perec, *L'Infra-ordinaire*, Seuil, 1989.

Claude Shannon, *"Programming a Computer for Playing chess"*, Philosophical Magazine, 7th series, 41, no. 314, 1950.

David Sheff, *Game Over: Press Start to Continue*, Cyberactive Media Group, 1999

Ben Shneiderman, *"Direct manipulation: a step beyond programming languages"*, IEEE Computer 16(8), 57-69, 1983.

I.M. Siegel, *"Nintendonitis"*, Orthopedics, 14, 1991.

Gilbert Simondon, *Du mode d'existence des objets techniques*, Persée, 1958.

Dean Takahashi, D. *Opening the Xbox: Inside Microsoft's Plan to Unleash an Entertainment Revolution*, Prima Press, 2002.

Mathieu Triclot, *Petite philosophie du jeu video, Zones*, Éditions La Découverte, 2011.

Alan Turing. *Solvable and Unsolvable Problems*, Science News, 31: 1954.

Ichiro Utsumi, *Nintendo. Gulliver Shôhô no Himitsu*, Nihon Bugeisham Tokyo, 1991.

John Vardalas, *"From DATAR To The FP-6000 Computer: Technological Change"*, In IEEE Annals of the History of Computing, Vol. 16, No.2, 1994.

Nicolas Villar, Kiel Mark Gilleade, Devina Ramduny-Ellis, Hans Gellersen, *"The VoodooIO gaming kit: a real-time adaptable gaming controller"*, Computers in Entertainment 5(3), 2007.

Paul Wexelblat, *PDP-1 Spacewar Reminiscences*, BBN, 1993.

Basile Zimmermann, *"Materiality, Description and Comparison as Tools for Cultural Difference Analysis"*, in Companion to New Media Dynamics, 2013.

Photos

Sony Playstation Control Pad - 1995

Sony Dual Analog Controller - 1997

Sony Dual Shock - 1998

Sony Dual Shock 3 - 2007

Super Nintendo - 1991

Nintendo NES-039 game controller - 1994

Philips CD-i - 1991

Nintendo Wii Classic - 2006

Mattel Intellivision - 1979

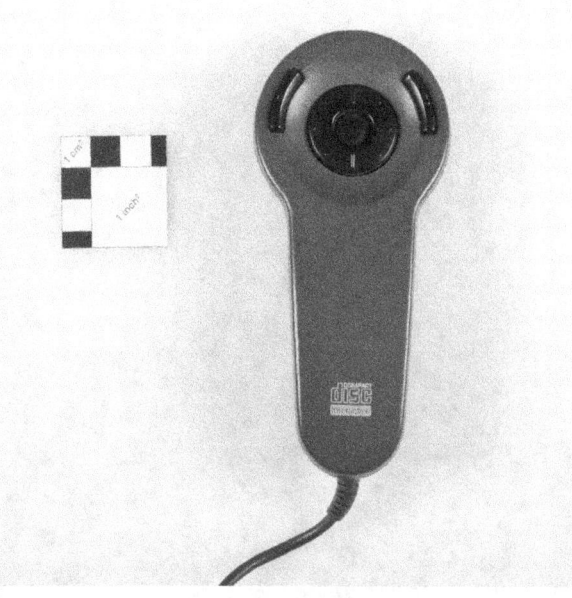

Philips CD-i - 1991

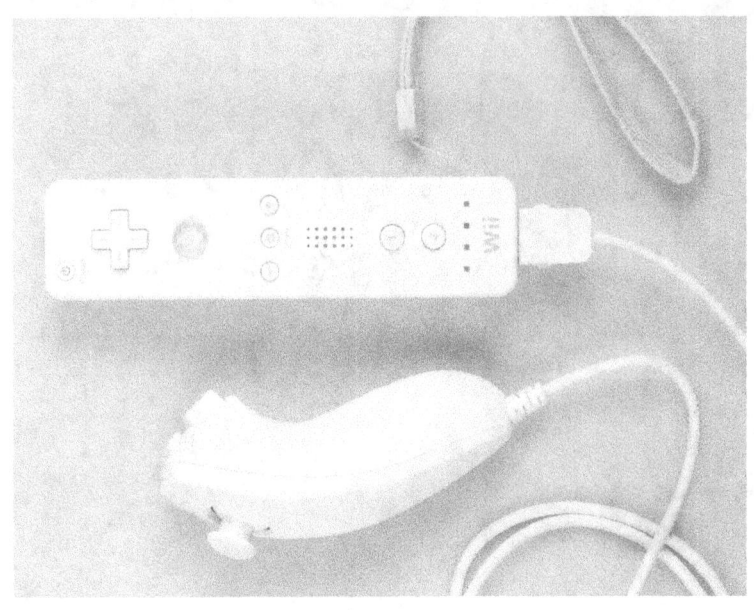

Nintendo Wiimote et Nunchuk - 2006

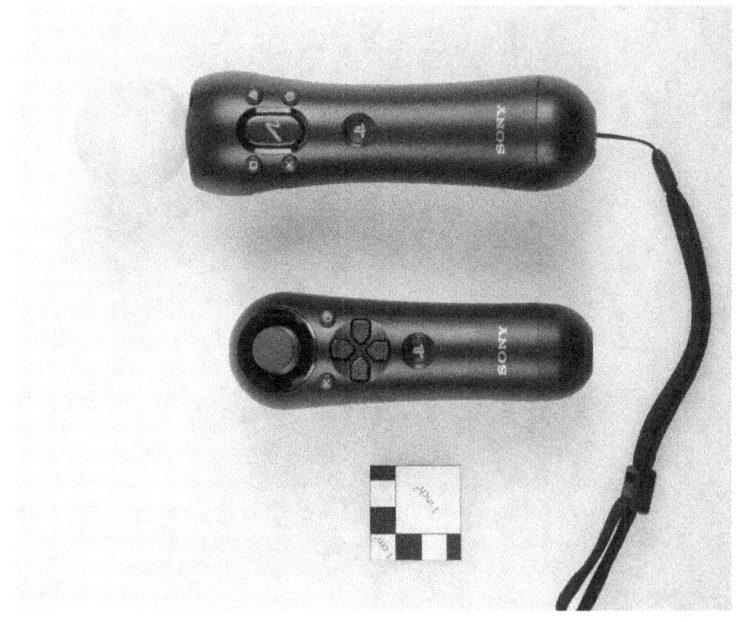

PlayStation Move - 2010

Nintendo Virtual Boy - 1995

Nintendo N64 controller (NUS-005) - 1996

Nintendo GameCube controller (DOL-003) - 2001

Nintendo Wii Classic Pro - 2009

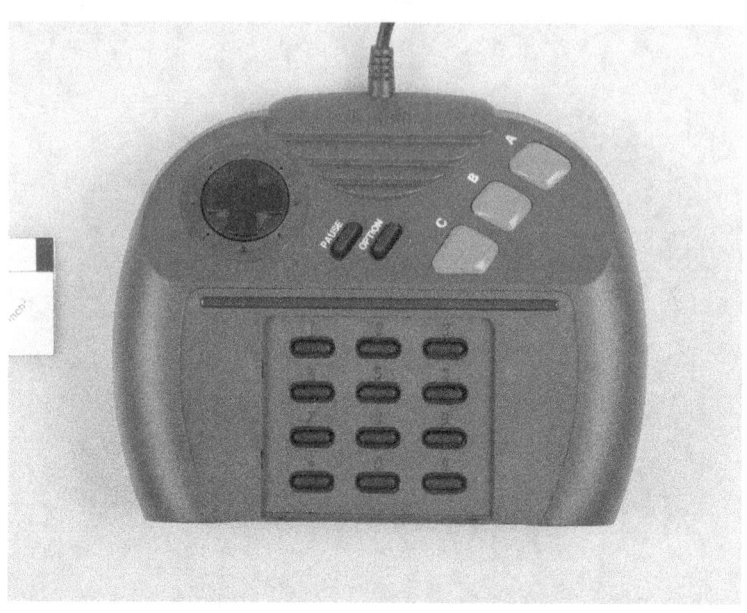

Atari Jaguar ProController - 1993

Sega Saturn 3D Pad - 1996

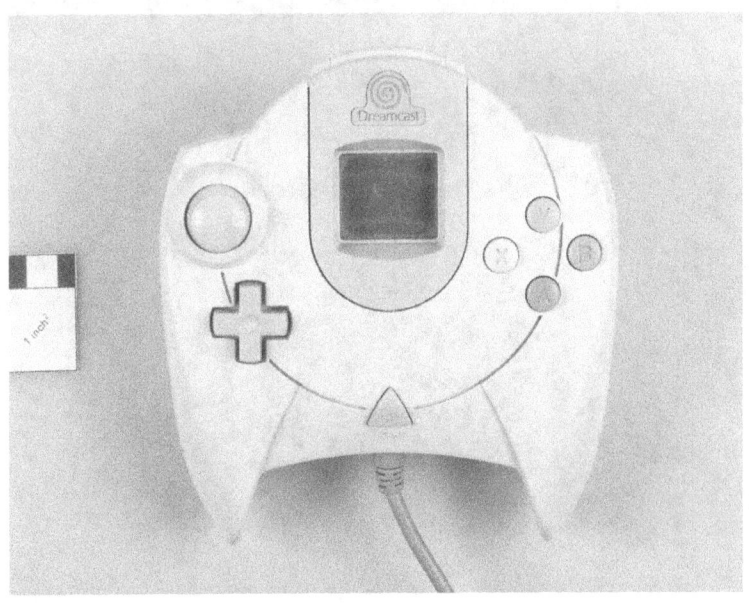

Sega Dreamcast controller - 1998

iQue Player - 2003

Microsoft Xbox controller - 2001

Microsoft Xbox controller S - 2002

Microsoft Xbox 360 controller - 2005

Nintendo Wii U Pro Controller - 2012

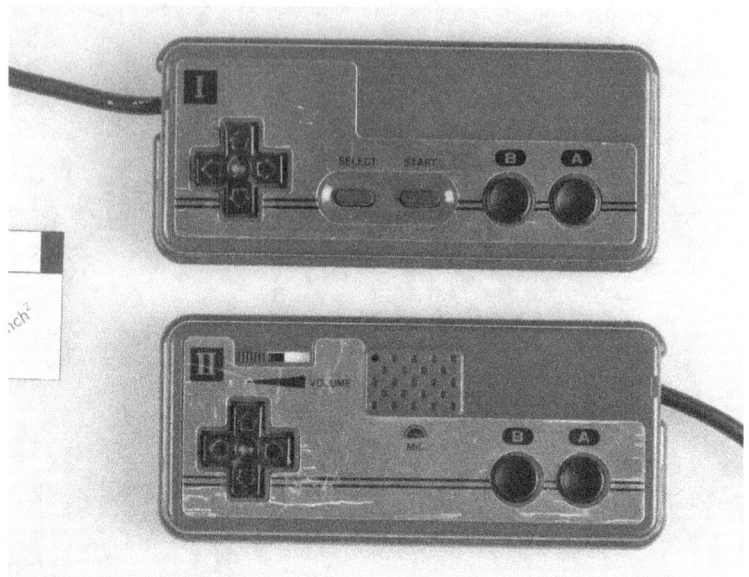

Nintendo Famicom – 1983

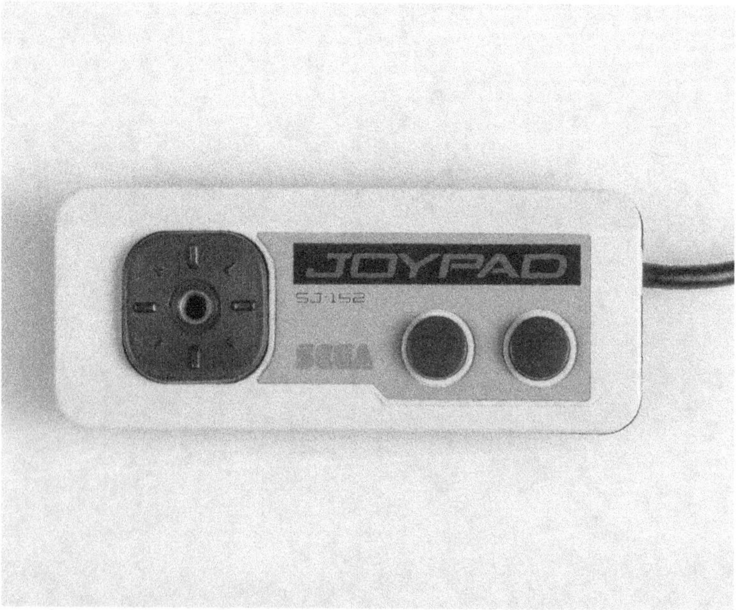

SEGA Mark III SJ-152 – 1985

Nintendo NES – 1985

SEGA Master System Controller – 1985

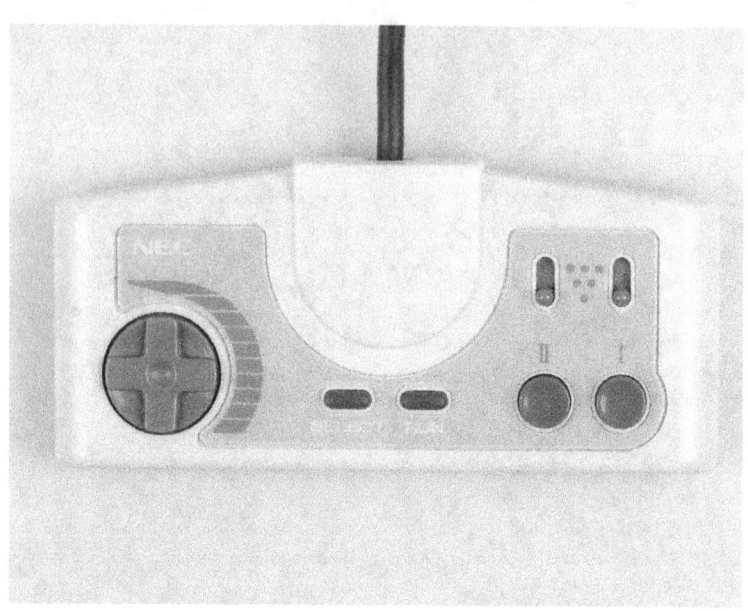

NEC PC Engine Controller - 1997

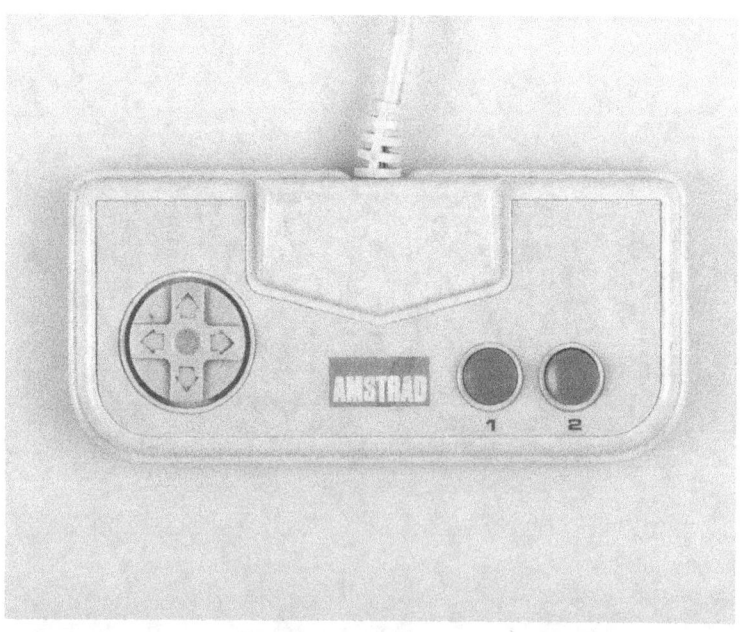

Amstrad GX4000 Controller - 1990

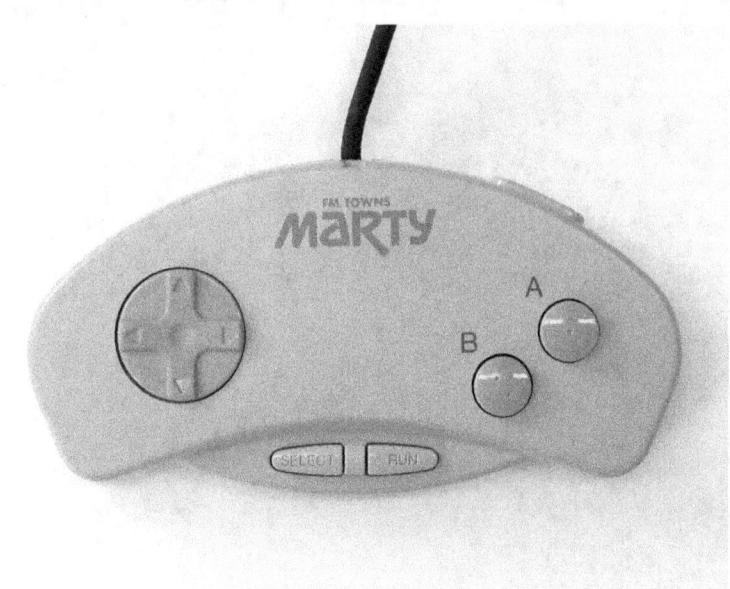

FM Towns Marty Controller - 1993

NEC PC-FX Controller - 1994

SEGA Mega Drive Control Pad II - 1988

SEGA Mega Drive Six Button Control pad - 1993

Panasonic 3DO Controller - 1993

Sega Saturn Model 1 controller - 1994

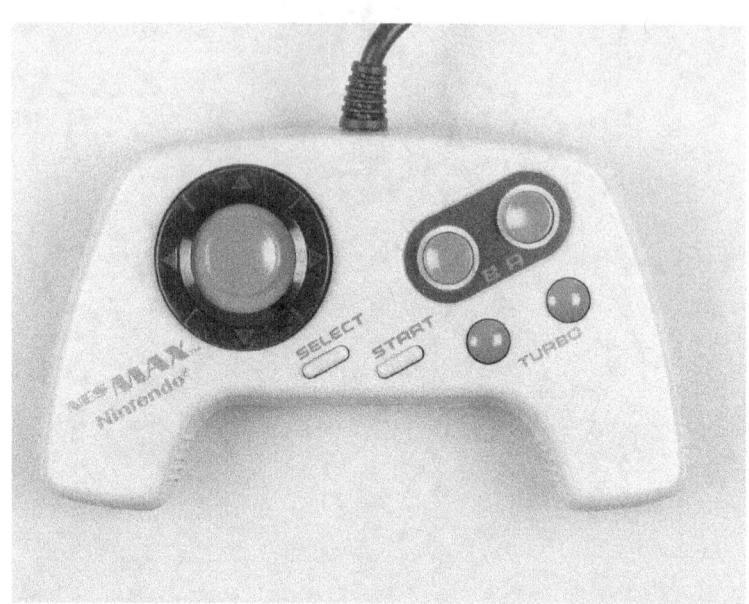

NES MAX- 1988

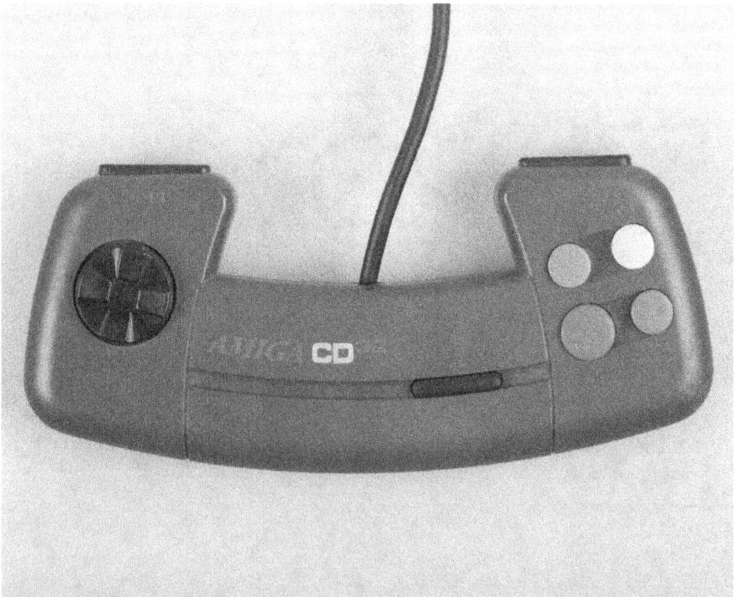

Amiga CD32 Controller - 1993

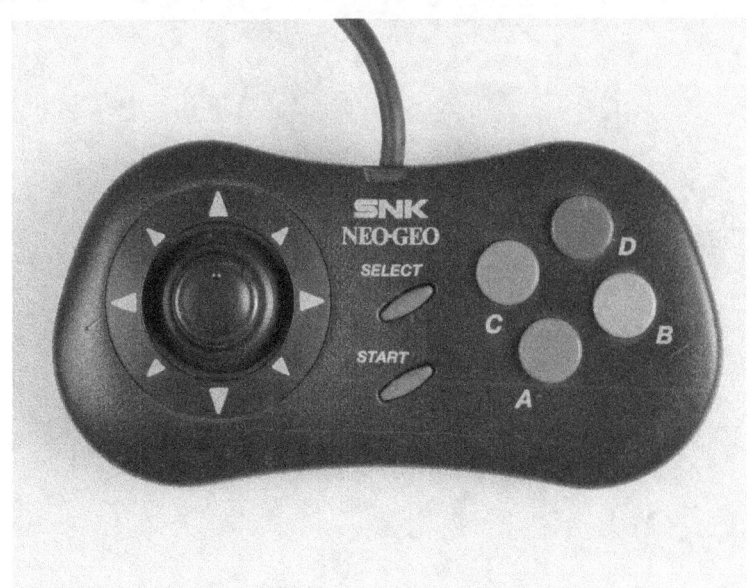

Neo Geo CD Controller - 1994

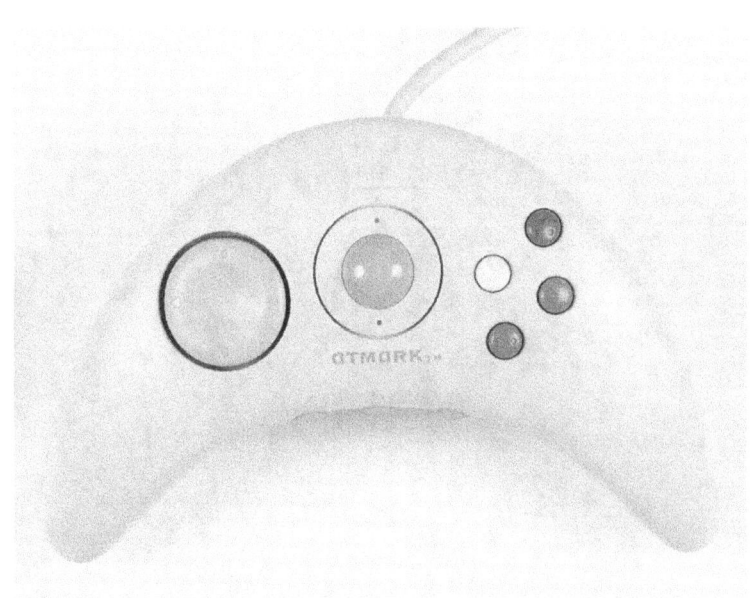

Pippin AppleJack controller - 1995

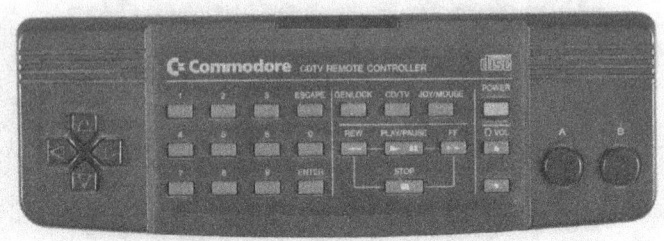

Commodore CDTV remote control/game pad - 1991

Nintendo Wii U GamePad - 2012

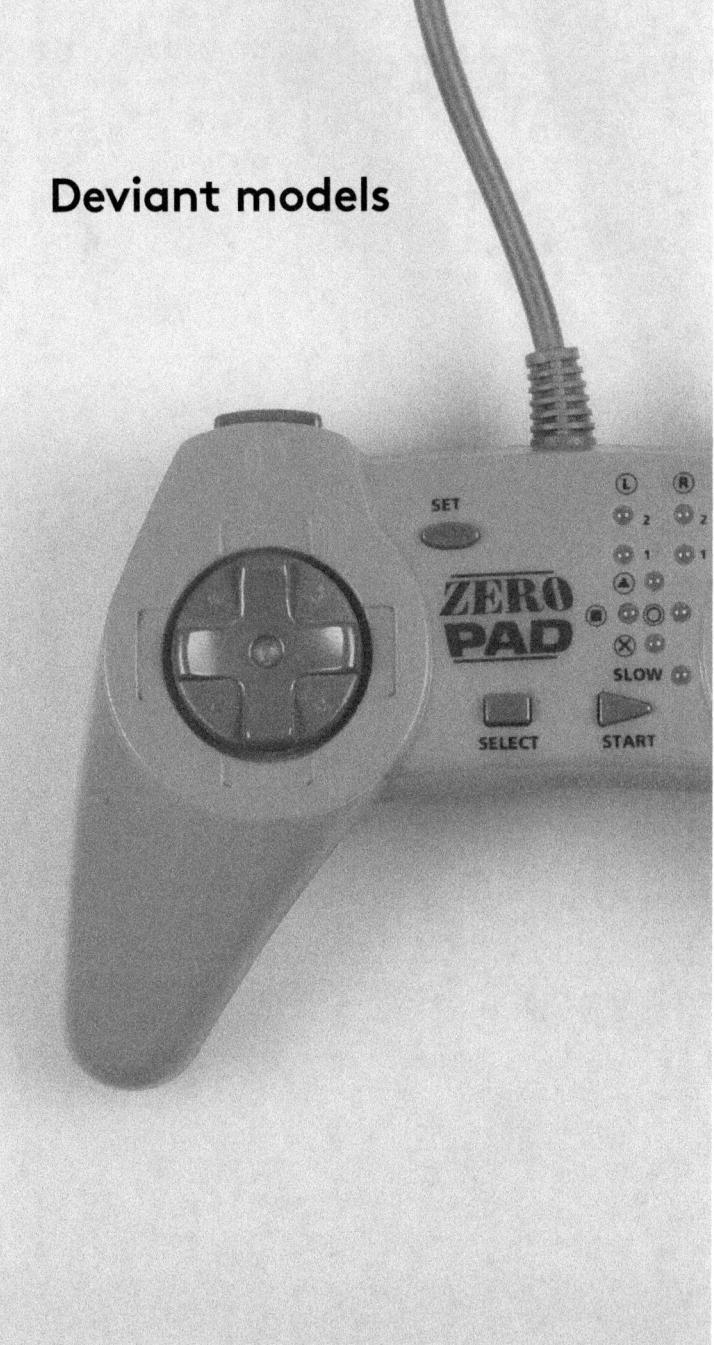

Deviant models

Namco NeGcon for PlayStation - 1995

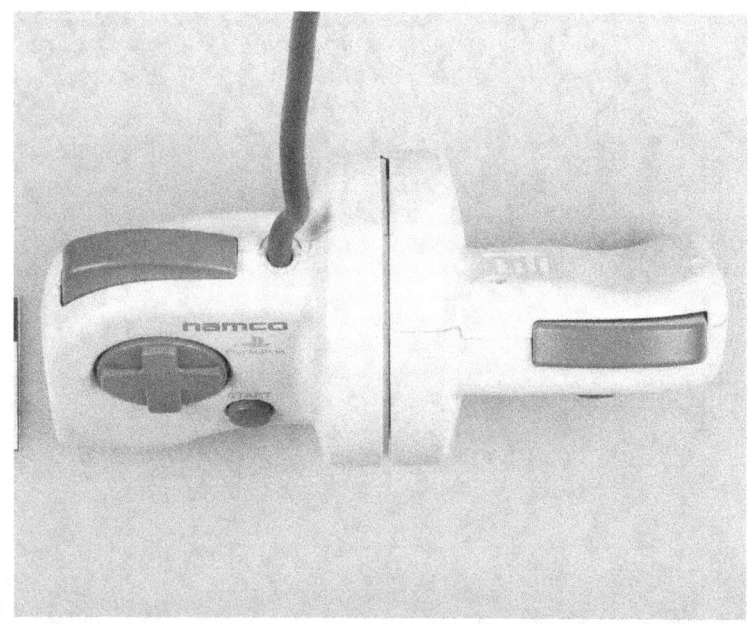

PS2 Controller Dragon Quest Slime - 2004

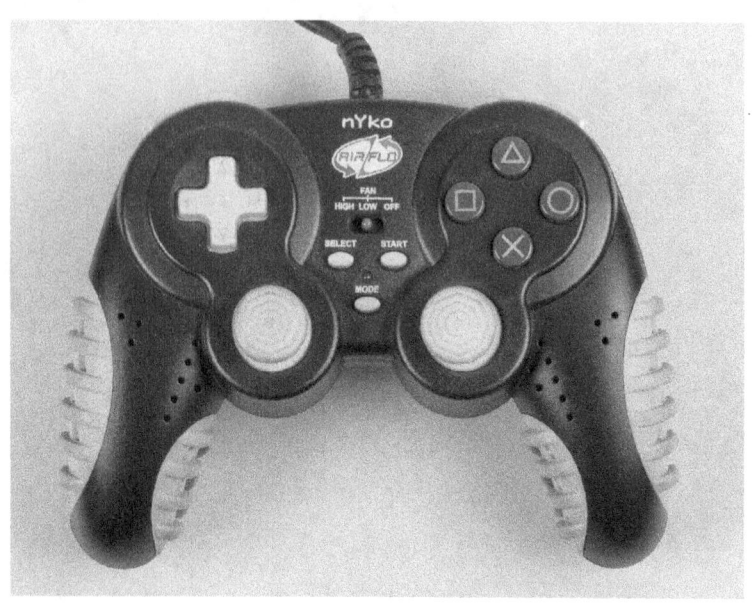

Nyko Airflo - 2002

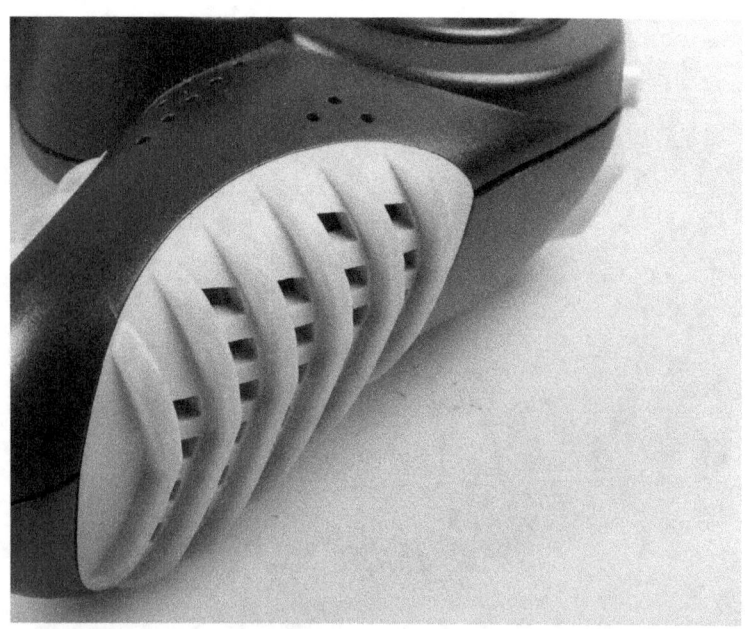

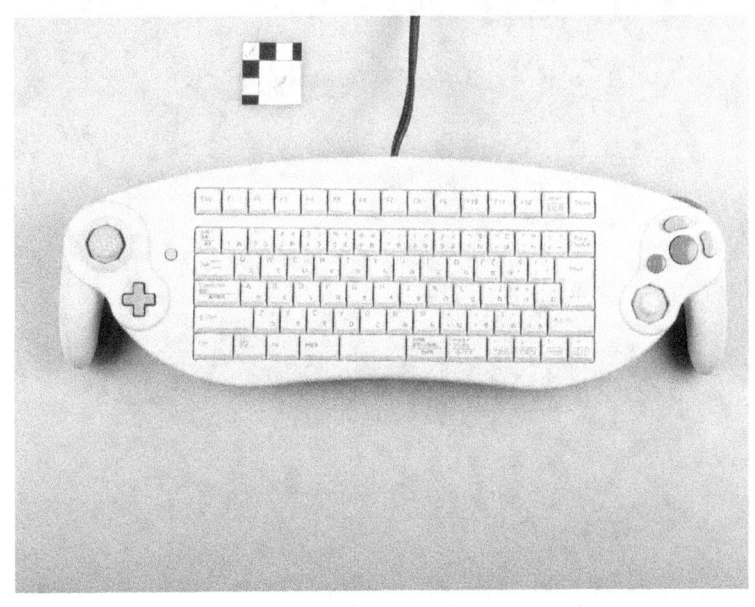

SAMMY GameCube Keyboard - 2003

RoydsPad PS2 controller - 2007

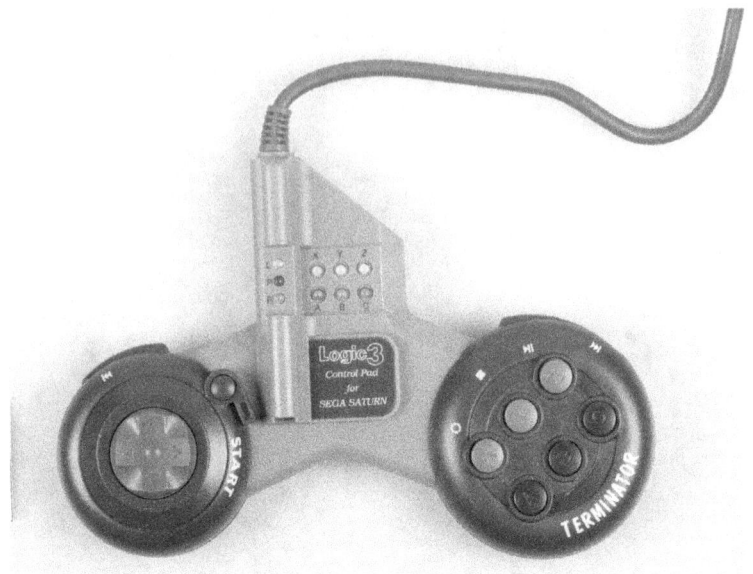

Logic 3 Terminator Controller for SEGA Saturn - 2003

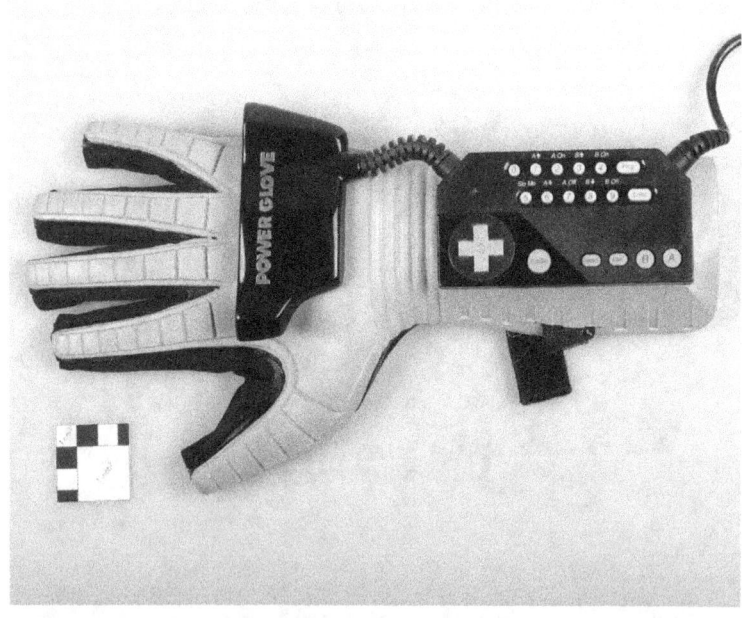

Mattel Power Glove for Nintendo Entertainment System (NES) –1989

Saturn Majoris AI – 1997

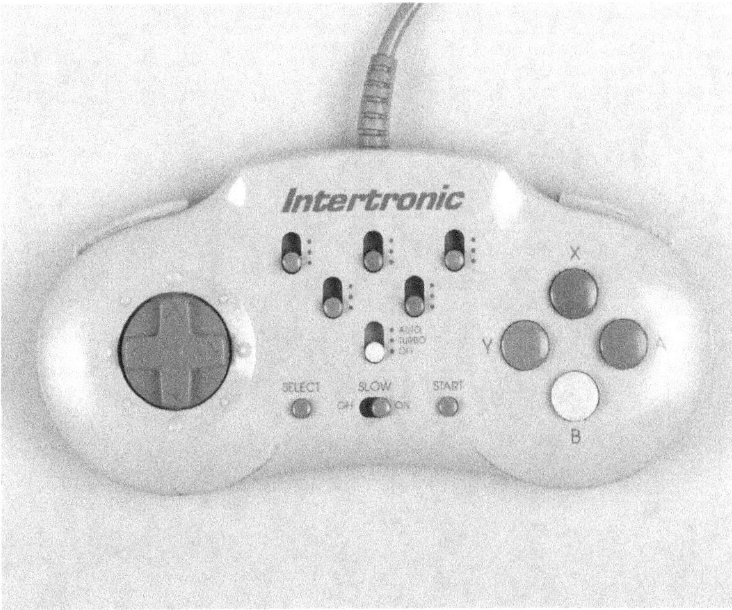

Intertronic Controller - 1992

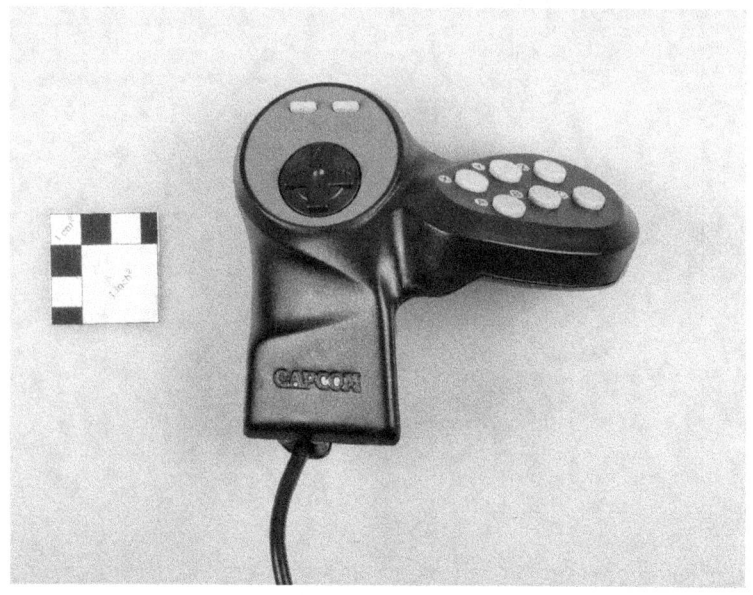

CAPCOM Pad soldier for Super Nintendo - 1994

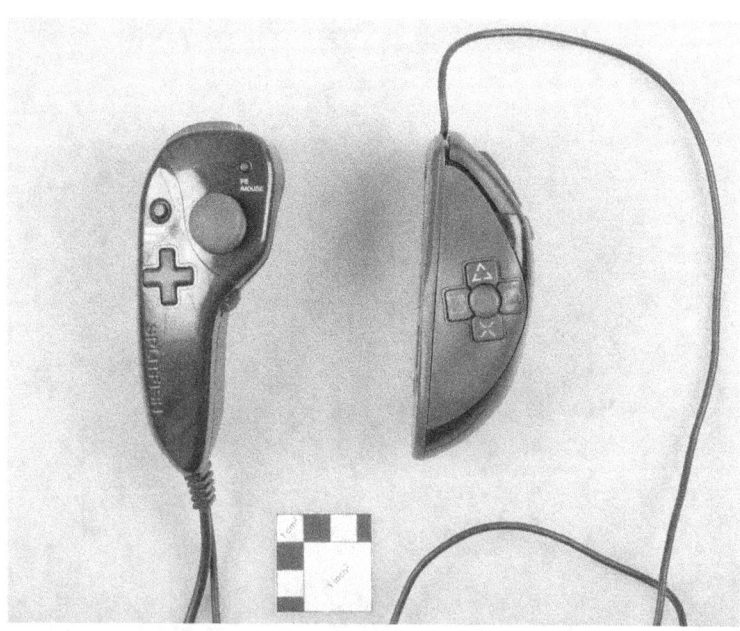

SplitFish FragFX for PS3 (mouse/joypad) - 2007

Logitech Wingman for PC - 1997

Rambo Stick Controller for SEGA Saturn - 1997